GOOD HOUSEKEEPING

MICROWAVE

Vegetarian

C O O K E R Y

GOOD HOUSEKEEPING

MICROWAVE

Vegetarian

COOKERY

JANET SMITH

EBURY PRESS, LONDON

Published by Ebury Press
Division of The National Magazine Company Limited
Colquhoun House
27–37 Broadwick Street
London W1V 1FR

First Impression 1987

ISBN 0 85223 696 4 (Hardback)
0 85223 691 3 (Paperback)

Editor Sue Wason
Designer Graham Dudley
Photographs by David Johnson
Photograph styling Kit Johnson
Food prepared for photography by Janet Smith

The author would specially like to thank Emma-Lee Gow for help with ideas and with
recipe testing.

Filmset by Advanced Filmsetters (Glasgow) Ltd
Printed and bound in Great Britain by Butler and Tanner Ltd, Frome and London

CONTENTS

INTRODUCTION

ALMOST VEGETARIAN

A meatless diet is no longer regarded as bizarre or cranky. Vegetarian eating has taken on new vitality and dimensions and now attracts over 1½ million people in this country. A further 2 million people have chosen to exclude red meat from their diet or to reduce their meat consumption in favour of meals based on vegetables, pasta or pulses. Recent nutritional studies show that we would all be healthier if we ate less fat, sugar and salt and increased our consumption of fibre-rich foods. A vegetarian or not quite vegetarian diet fits perfectly into this way of thinking.

Demi-veg is the name given to the new style of eating that's not quite vegetarian. Awareness of the need for a healthy diet and worries about additives in processed foods, and hormone treatments given to animals, means that many people are now choosing to cut down on fats, sugar and salt by eating leaner meats such as chicken, low-fat dairy products and more fruit and vegetables.

Although all the recipes in this book are vegetarian, they are invaluable to the demi-veg wanting to expand culinary horizons.

WHY VEGETARIAN?

Like those choosing a demi-veg diet many people decide to eat a vegetarian diet purely for health reasons. Current thinking is that many so-called 'diseases of Western civilisation' such as heart disease, strokes, obesity and high blood pressure are related to a conventional diet high in animal fats, sugar and salt and low in fibre. A vegetarian diet replaces all animal fats with vegetable ones and usually cuts down on the total intake.

Health reasons apart, some vegetarians dislike the idea of rearing and slaughtering animals for food. They are concerned about the environment and consider that eating meat squanders precious acres of farmland, when sufficient food could be grown on a fraction of the area needed for livestock and their feed.

Vegans choose not to eat any animal foods for either or both of these reasons. They exclude eggs, all dairy produce and sometimes honey from their diets.

BALANCING A VEGETARIAN DIET

Until recently most of us were brought up to expect a meal of the 'meat and two veg' type, so changing to a meat-free diet can be difficult in terms of what to eat with what in order to balance flavours as well as nutrients. There are no rules to follow regarding what should be eaten with what. This book contains soups, savouries and snacks, dips, terrines, salads, pasta, grains, noodles and pickles as well as hearty feasts, puddings and baking—a wide variety of dishes suitable for combining in various ways. Try a meal of dips and breads followed by a salad or a hearty feast and a grain dish. Soups can be eaten before a main course, as part of it or, in the case of fruit soups, after it as a dessert. Terrines can be eaten hot with vegetable accompaniments or cold with salad and pickles. Meals become more interesting when a selection of well-flavoured dishes are eaten together as one course, in the style of China or India. Tasty side dishes such as pickles, juicy black olives marinated in olive oil and garlic, roasted nuts or raitas flavoured with spices, cucumber or fresh mint, make simple but effective contributions to any meal. When entertaining I like to offer one or two main dishes such as terrines or mousses, or hearty feasts, accompanied by a grain or pulse dish, a salad and a selection of these small dishes. The permutations are endless—the only boundaries being your personal likes and dislikes.

As long as a good variety of foods is eaten, a meatless diet provides all the foods our bodies need. However, a basic understanding of the main food groups and why they are necessary is helpful.

PROTEIN

Meat eaters often live under the misconception that protein only comes from 'a good piece of steak'. In fact there are lots of vegetable sources of protein such as beans, grains and nuts.

Protein is made up of smaller units called amino acids. These form about 75 per cent of the body's solid mass and are needed in every cell, so they are very important. The body can make certain amino acids itself, but others, known as the essential amino acids, must come from food. The protein in animal foods such as meat contains roughly all of the necessary amino acids. This could explain why meat protein has always been regarded as superior to vegetable protein. Protein from a vegetable source lacks or is low in one or more of the essential amino acids. However, one source of vegetable protein can make up for the deficiency in others. So by eating certain foods together they can be balanced to make complete proteins. For example, grains should be eaten with dairy products or beans (muesli with milk, bean casserole with rice) and nuts should be eaten with beans (bean and nut roast). Soya is the exception to this rule and is a source of protein similar to the kind obtained from meat. So soya beans and soya products such as tofu, soya milk and soya flour are good protein-rich foods for the vegetarian.

CARBOHYDRATES AND FIBRE

These are important suppliers of energy to the body and, although in the past people were often advised to cut down on carbohydrates as a means of controlling weight, research has shown that everyone should be eating more foods which are high in the *unrefined* carbohydrates, such as wholemeal bread, wholemeal flour and brown rice. When these are refined into white bread, flour and rice most of the dietary fibre is removed, reducing their food value.

Dietary fibre, known as roughage, is found only in plant foods, where it gives structure to plant cell walls. It is indigestible and remains in the intestine after the nutrients have been absorbed. Although it is of no nutritional value, it plays a vital role in keeping the body healthy. It prevents constipation and may also prevent certain diseases of the intestine, such as diverticulosis, cancer of the large bowel and possibly other disorders like varicose veins and heart disease, although this has yet to be proved.

Dietary fibre works by holding a lot of water. The more fibre that is eaten, the most moisture is absorbed and it becomes easy for the intestine to push the soft, bulky waste matter along without pressure or straining. It also means that any potentially harmful substances are diluted and eliminated quickly from the body, spending little time in contact with the wall of the intestine.

Increasing fibre intake doesn't mean adding bran to everything. It is much better to eat more foods that are naturally high in fibre, like wholegrain cereals (including wholemeal and brown bread which include brans or fibres), wholegrain breakfast cereals, muesli, wholewheat pasta and rice, fruit, vegetables and pulses. An excess of uncooked bran can reduce the absorption of zinc and certain other minerals but an adult would have to eat quite a bit for this to happen. Children under the age of two, however, should not be given uncooked bran.

SUGAR

This is the one carbohydrate that everyone should cut down on. It is a very concentrated form of energy— 10 ml (2 tsp) contains around 40 calories. It has few nutrients and little bulk, which means it is easy to eat large amounts.

There is no significant nutritional difference between refined white sugar and brown sugar; both are detrimental to teeth. It's particularly damaging in sticky forms like cakes, sweets and biscuits and the more often it's eaten the more damage it does, so frequent sugary snacks are worse than the same amount of sugar in one meal.

Replace them with fresh fruit, salad or vegetables and use fruit purées to sweeten cakes.

SALT

Salt is a compound of sodium and chloride, both of which are minerals essential for regulating the amount of water in body cells and transmitting nervous impulses. Chloride also produces hydrochloric acid in the stomach, which aids digestion, and sodium is important for muscle contraction and the regulation of blood pressure.

Sodium occurs naturally in many foods and is also added in the form of salt or other sodium-containing compounds. It has important implications for health. The theory is that a high sodium intake is an important factor in the development of high blood pressure (hypertension) in certain susceptible individuals. In communities where salt intake is very low, so too is the incidence of high blood pressure. In Japan, where salt intake is very high, roughly 40 per cent of middle-aged adults have high blood pressure.

High blood pressure is a major risk factor in the development of heart and blood vessel disease and greatly increases the risk of heart attacks and strokes. Nutritionists and many within the medical profession feel the evidence is strong enough to recommend that we cut down on the amount of salt we eat. However, other experts claim there is not enough evidence 7 available to justify recommending major changes to our diet.

Approximately 70 per cent of the salt we eat is present in food, much of it added during manufacture. The other 30 per cent is added at the table or in cooking. Try to reduce this by using other flavourings such as spices. Vegetables cooked in the microwave should not have salt added before cooking—try to educate yourself not to add it after cooking either.

FAT AND CHOLESTEROL

Small amounts of fats are necessary to health, but most of us eat far more than our bodies require.

Fats can be divided into three categories: saturated, monosaturated and polyunsaturated. Saturated fats are mainly found in meats and dairy products; they tend to increase the amount of cholesterol in the blood. The body manufactures its own supply of cholesterol in the liver, as a certain amount is essential to make bile acids and various hormones. However, excess cholesterol in the blood can lead to heart disease.

As well as its own manufactured supply, the body uses both cholesterol and saturated fats from foods to make blood cholesterol. Of the two, saturated fats have the most impact on blood cholesterol.

Monosaturated fats have no effect on blood cholesterol—they neither raise nor lower it. They include the fats in avocados, cashew nuts, olives and olive oil, peanuts and peanut butter.

Polyunsaturated fats may lower the level of cholesterol in the blood and could protect against heart disease. These fats are usually liquid at room temperature, such as corn oil, safflower oil, sesame oil and sunflower oil. Some margarines are high in poly-unsaturated fat and are recommended by most nutritionists as a healthy alternative to those high in saturated fats.

From the point of view of weight control, it is best to cut down on *all* fats and eat more bread, cereals, fresh fruit and vegetables.

VITAMINS AND OTHER NUTRIENTS

Vitamins, which are vital for proper body functioning, can be divided into two different types—the fat-soluble and the water-soluble ones. Vitamins A, D, E and K dissolve in fats and are mostly found in foods which contain fat. They are stored in the liver in amounts large enough to last for several months. The water-soluble vitamins, C and the B complex, dissolve in water and cannot be stored in the body in large quantities. Small amounts are found in body cells and added together they form what nutritionists call the vitamin pool. Once the pool is full or saturated, any

excess is simply excreted from the body. As the vitamins are used up, the pool needs to be topped up.

Eating a wide variety of foods should ensure your body gets all the vitamins, protein and other nutrients it needs. Unhealthy eating habits could, however, mean you are going short of certain vitamins and minerals. Although vitamin supplements are unlikely to do any harm, they are not the best answer to poor eating habits.

How to make the most of vitamins

Cooking in the microwave minimizes vitamin and mineral losses because they are cooked quickly in small amounts of water. Leave the skins on when you can and eat vegetables and fruit raw whenever possible. Vitamin losses continue after cooking, particularly when warm foods are left waiting around, so eat as soon as possible. Water-soluble vitamin C and B-group vitamins arc easily lost or destroyed during storage, preparation and cooking. Choose fruit and vegetables in peak condition, store them in a cool dry place and eat as soon as possible. Tough, old vegetables have a lower vitamin content than fresh, and even the microwave won't revive their texture.

Vitamins and microwave cooking

Rapid microwave cooking times mean that fewer vitamins are destroyed. Most foods cook in their own juices or need only small amounts of water to keep them moist which means there is less likelihood that vitamins and minerals will leach out and be lost in the cooking water. Foods like fruit and vegetables can be cooked just before you need them and eaten immediately, before the vitamin content dwindles. A short burst in the microwave will yield more vitamin C-rich juice from citrus fruits. Precooked meals and leftovers can be chilled or frozen and reheated in the microwave with little loss of vitamins. The microwave is also ideal for blanching fruit and vegetables for the freezer.

GUIDE TO VITAMINS

Folic acid

Needed to produce healthy red blood cells. Deficiency causes a form of anaemia.
Good food sources green leafy vegetables, pulses, wholemeal bread, cereals and oranges.

Pantothenic acid

Plays an important role in releasing energy from fat and carbohydrate.
Good food sources found in a wide variety of foods. Eggs, cheese and nuts are particularly rich sources.

Thiamin (Vitamin B1)

Helps to release energy from carbohydrates.
Good food sources milk, eggs, fruit, vegetables, wholegrain and fortified cereals including bread and breakfast cereals, pulses, nuts.

Riboflavin (Vitamin B2)

Needed for releasing energy from foods.
Good food sources milk, eggs, cheese and yeast extract.

Niacin

Helps with the conversion of food to release energy.
Good food sources fortified breakfast cereals, vegetables and yeast extract.

Pyridoxin (Vitamin B6)

Helps the body utilise protein and is important for the formation of healthy red blood cells.
Good food sources cereals, pulses.

Cobalamin (Vitamin B12)

Essential for the formation of healthy red blood cells. Deficiency causes a form of anaemia. Vegans may be at risk of deficiency and should eat fortified foods or take supplements.
Good food sources eggs, milk and cheese. Some foods are fortified with this vitamin.

Biotin

Essential for the metabolism of fat.
Good food sources eggs, vegetables, cereals, fruit and nuts. It is also made by naturally occurring bacteria in the intestine.

Vitamin C (Ascorbic acid)

Needed for healthy connective tissue. Claims that large doses prevent or cure colds are unproven. Smokers, oral contraceptive users and people recovering from surgery have higher requirements.
Good food sources fresh fruit, particularly citrus fruits and blackcurrants, and vegetables, including potatoes.

Vitamin A (Retinol)

Needed for growth, good vision in dim light, healthy skin and surface tissues. Retinol is the active form of vitamin A but other substances in food including carotene can be converted into vitamin A by the body.
Good food sources dairy foods, green leafy vegetables, yellow and orange fruits and vegetables such as carrots, tomatoes and peaches, butter and margarine.

Vitamin D (Cholecalciferol)

Needed for growth and the formation of healthy teeth and bones. Most of the body's supply comes from the action of sunlight on a substance in the skin.
Good food sources eggs, butter. Margarine, some milk powders and yogurts are fortified with Vitamin D.

Vitamin E

Thought to be essential for muscular health and blood circulation.
Good food sources wheat germ, vegetable oils, some root vegetables, green leafy vegetables, cereals and nuts.

Vitamin K

Needed for the normal clotting of blood.
Good food sources cereals, pulses and green leafy vegetables. Some is also manufactured by bacteria in the intestine.

MINERALS

These cannot be manufactured by the body and must be obtained from food. At present, 15 minerals have been identified as being essential to health and others are still under investigation. The majority of people obtain enough minerals provided a good variety of food is eaten.

Calcium is essential for the growth and development of bones, teeth and tissues. It is also needed for muscle contraction, nerve functioning, the action of several enzymes and for the normal clotting of blood. Calcium is found in milk, yogurt, cheese (including reduced and low-fat varieties), white or brown bread and flour (which are fortified with calcium), eggs and green vegetables.

Iron is used to make the haemoglobin in red blood cells and is stored in the muscles and liver. Haemoglobin carries oxygen to supply all the body's cells and a shortage leads to anaemia. Iron deficiency is fairly common in Britain, particularly in women of child-bearing age, since iron requirements are increased by menstrual loss and pregnancy.

The body can adapt to increased needs by increasing its absorption from the intestine, but some women still need to be prescribed iron tablets or supplements. Iron is found in cereals, pulses and vegetables. Vitamin C increases the absorption of iron from all foods.

Magnesium is concentrated in the bones and provides strength for them. Minute amounts are also found in body cells. It is necessary for the functioning of some enzymes and also plays a part in breaking down foods to release energy. It is found in cocoa, some nuts and green vegetables.

Phosphorus is mainly laid down in the skeleton with calcium. The rest interacts with some B complex vitamins to release energy from foods and is present in small quantities in many body cells. It is found in a wide variety of foods.

9

Potassium, together with sodium, plays a vital part in the functioning of nerves and in determining blood pressure. It is found in many foods, particularly fruit, vegetables, cereals, eggs and cheese.

Sulphur is found in minute quantities in every cell in the body. All protein foods contain sulphur, so there is no danger of deficiency.

Trace elements are mineral substances present in the body in very small amounts. With the varied diet eaten in Britain, there is unlikely to be a deficiency of any of the important ones known so far. Considerable work is being done on trace elements and new ones may well yet emerge. Those recognised as being essential for health include cobalt, copper, chromium, fluoride, iodine, manganese and zinc.

COOKING VEGETABLES IN THE MICROWAVE OVEN

Cooking vegetables is simple and quick as long as you forget all about conventional cooking. Because microwave cooking is a moist method of cooking, foods can be cooked in little or no added water. In most cases 30 ml (2 tbsp) water is adequate, adding larger amounts only slows down cooking and produces slushy, overcooked vegetables.

COOKING FRESH VEGETABLES

When using this chart add 30 ml (2 tbsp) water unless otherwise stated. The vegetables can be cooked in boil-in-the-bags, plastic containers and polythene bags—pierce the bag before cooking to make sure there is a space for steam to escape.

Prepare vegetables in the normal way. It is most important that food is cut to an even size and stems are of the same length. Vegetables with skins, such as aubergines, need to be pierced before microwaving to prevent bursting. Season vegetables with salt after cooking if required. Salt distorts the microwave patterns and dries the vegetables.

Vegetable	Quantity	Approximate time on HIGH	Microwave Cooking Technique(s)
Artichoke, globe	1 2 3 4	5–6 minutes 7–8 minutes 11–12 minutes 12–13 minutes	*Place* upright in covered dish.
Asparagus	450 g (1 lb)	7–8 minutes	*Place* stalks towards the outside of the dish. *Re-position* during cooking.
Aubergine	450 g (1 lb) 0.5 cm (¼ inch) slices	5–6 minutes	*Stir* or *shake* after 4 minutes.
Beans, broad	450 g (1 lb)	6–8 minutes	*Stir* or *shake* after 3 minutes and test after 5 minutes.
Beans, green	450 g (1 lb) sliced into 2.5 cm (1 inch) lengths	10–13 minutes	*Stir* or *shake* during the cooking period. Time will vary with age.
Beetroot, whole	4 medium	14–16 minutes	*Pierce* skin with a fork. *Re-position* during cooking.
Broccoli	450 g (1 lb) small florets.	7–8 minutes	*Re-position* during cooking. *Place* stalks towards the outside of the dish.
Brussels sprouts	225 g (8 oz) 450 g (1 lb)	4–6 minutes 7–10 minutes	*Stir* or *shake* during cooking.
Cabbage	450 g (1 lb) quartered 450 g (1 lb) shredded	8 minutes 8–10 minutes	*Stir* or *shake* during cooking.
Carrots	450 g (1 lb) small whole 450 g (1 lb) 0.5 cm (¼ inch) slices	8–10 minutes 9–12 minutes	*Stir* or *shake* during cooking.
Cauliflower	whole 450 g (1 lb) 225 g (8 oz) florets 450 g (1 lb) florets	9–12 minutes 5–6 minutes 7–8 minutes	*Stir* or *shake* during cooking.

Celery	450 g (1 lb) sliced into 2.5 cm (1 inch) lengths	8–10 minutes	*Stir* or *shake* during cooking.
Corn-on-the-cob	2 cobs 450 g (1 lb)	6–7 minutes	*Wrap* individually in greased greaseproof paper. *Do not* add water. *Turn* over after 3 minutes.
Courgettes	450 g (1 lb) 2.5 cm (1 inch) slices	5–7 minutes	*Do not* add more than 30 ml (2 tbsp) water. *Stir* or *shake* gently twice during cooking. *Stand* for 2 minutes before draining.
Fennel	450 g (1 lb) 0.5 cm ($\frac{1}{4}$ inch) slices	7–9 minutes	*Stir* and *shake* during cooking.
Leeks	450 g (1 lb) 2.5 cm (1 inch) slices	6–8 minutes	*Stir* or *shake* during cooking.
Mangetout	450 g (1 lb)	7–9 minutes	*Stir* or *shake* during cooking.
Mushrooms	225 g (8 oz) whole 450 g (1 lb) whole	2–3 minutes 5 minutes	*Do not* add water. Add 25 g (1 oz) butter or alternative fat and a squeeze of lemon juice. *Stir* or *shake* gently during cooking.
Onions	225 g (8 oz) thinly sliced. 450 g (1 lb) small whole	7–8 minutes 9–11 minutes	*Stir* or *shake* sliced onions. *Add only* 60 ml (4 tbsp) water to whole onions. *Re-position* whole onions during cooking.
Okra	450 g (1 lb) whole	6–8 minutes	*Stir* or *shake* during cooking.
Parsnips	450 g (1 lb) halved	10–16 minutes	*Place* thinner parts towards the centre. *Add* a knob of butter and 15 ml (1 tbsp) lemon juice with 150 ml ($\frac{1}{4}$ pint) water. *Turn* dish during cooking and *re-position*.
Peas	450 g (1 lb)	9–11 minutes	*Stir* or *shake* during cooking.
Potatoes Baked jacket	 1 × 175 g (6 oz) potato 2 × 175 g (6 oz) potatoes 4 × 175 g (6 oz) potatoes	 4–6 minutes 6–8 minutes 12–14 minutes	*Wash* and prick the skin with a fork. *Place* on absorbent kitchen paper or napkin. *When* cooking more than two at a time arrange in a circle. *Turn* over halfway through cooking.
Boiled (old) halved	450 g (1 lb)	7–10 minutes	*Add* 60 ml (4 tbsp) water. *Stir* or *shake* during cooking.
Boiled (new) whole	450 g (1 lb)	6–9 minutes	*Add* 60 ml (4 tbsp) water. *Do not* overcook or new potatoes become spongy.
Sweet	450 g (1 lb)	5 minutes	*Wash* and prick the skin with a fork. *Place* on absorbent kitchen paper. *Turn* over halfway through cooking time.
Spinach	450 g (1 lb) chopped	5–6 minutes	*Do not* add water. Best cooked in roasting bag, sealed with non-metal fastening. *Stir* or *shake* during cooking.
Swede	450 g (1 lb) 2 cm ($\frac{3}{4}$ inch) dice	11–13 minutes	*Stir* or *shake* during cooking.
Turnip	450 g (1 lb) 2 cm ($\frac{3}{4}$ inch) dice	9–11 minutes	*Add* 60 ml (4 tbsp) water and *stir* or *shake* during cooking.

COOKING FROZEN VEGETABLES

Frozen vegetables may be cooked straight from the freezer. Many may be cooked in their original plastic packaging, as long as it is first slit and then placed on a plate. Alternatively, transfer to a bowl.

Vegetable	Quantity	Approximate time on HIGH	Microwave Cooking Technique(s)
Asparagus	275 g (10 oz)	7–9 minutes	*Separate* and re-arrange after 3 minutes.
Beans, broad	225 g (8 oz)	7–8 minutes	*Stir* or *shake* during cooking period.
Beans, green cut	225 g (8 oz)	6–8 minutes	*Stir* or *shake* during cooking period.
Broccoli	275 g (10 oz)	7–9 minutes	*Re-arrange* spears after 3 minutes.
Brussels sprouts	225 g (8 oz)	6–8 minutes	*Stir* or *shake* during cooking period.
Cauliflower florets	275 g (10 oz)	7–9 minutes	*Stir* or *shake* during cooking period.
Carrots	225 g (8 oz)	6–7 minutes	*Stir* or *shake* during cooking period.
Corn-on-the-cob	1 2	3–4 minutes 6–7 minutes	*Do not* add water. Dot with butter, wrap in greaseproof paper.
Mixed vegetables	225 g (8 oz)	5–6 minutes	*Stir* or *shake* during cooking period.
Peas	225 g (8 oz)	5–6 minutes	*Stir* or *shake* during cooking period.
Peas and carrots	225 g (8 oz)	7–8 minutes	*Stir* or *shake* during cooking period.
Spinach, leaf or chopped	275 g (10 oz)	7–9 minutes	*Do not* add water. *Stir* or *shake* during cooking period.
Swede and Turnip, diced	225 g (8 oz)	6–7 minutes	*Stir* or *shake* during cooking period. *Mash* with butter after standing time.
Sweetcorn	225 g (8 oz)	4–6 minutes	*Stir* or *shake* during cooking period.

Because less water is used, vegetables and fruits lose fewer vitamins and minerals when cooked in a microwave oven (in conventional cooking, water-soluble vitamins are leached into the cooking water). Baking vegetables, such as potatoes, yams, aubergines, whole, means that maximum vitamins are retained. Whole vegetables should be pricked before cooking to prevent them bursting.

Delicate green vegetables such as courgettes, broccoli, green beans and mangetouts cook very quickly. They should all be served while still crunchy and bright green in colour.

Tougher root vegetables take longer to cook and need more water. The cooking time depends on the thickness of slices or size of chunks; always cut into even-sized pieces and stir to ensure even cooking. Baked potatoes are one of the great triumphs of the microwave oven and ideal for quick vegetarian meals (see page 40), taking a quarter or a third of the conventional cooking time. I like to bake potatoes whole in the microwave oven and then scoop out the cooked potato flesh to mix with nuts, cheese and herbs or spices to make burgers, or to use whenever mashed potato is required.

If you want to cook a mixture of vegetables, it is important to choose those that need the same cooking time, for example carrots and parsnips, or cook one slightly in the oven before adding the other.

The microwave oven is ideal for cooking smaller or individual portions of vegetables. Simply put them in a small bowl or on a plate with no more than 15 ml (1 tbsp) water. Cover and cook on HIGH for about 2 minutes or until tender.

Stir-fries convert well to microwave cooking. Although not true stir-fries, a mixture of colourful vegetables cut into matchstick strips cooks to perfection in just 2–3 minutes, ready for flavouring with ginger, soy sauce, oils or herbs.

COOKING PULSES

Dried pulses toughen with age so buy in small quantities and use within nine months. Store in airtight containers in a cool dark place as damp can spoil the flavour and may encourage mould. Sunlight changes the colour and flavour so those stored in glass jars should be used within three months.

The weight of dried pulses approximately doubles during cooking, so if a recipe states 225 g (8 oz) cooked beans you will need to start with 100 g (4 oz). A 425 g (14 oz) can of beans, drained, is equal to 225 g (8 oz) cooked beans. Although canned beans often have sugar and salt added and usually have a much softer texture than freshly cooked beans, they are a good quick alternative to cooking your own.

Red kidney beans, soya beans, haricot beans, navy beans, black beans and lima beans contain toxins that can cause stomach upsets. To destroy the toxins, the beans should be boiled rapidly for 10 minutes. These beans, as well as borlotti beans, cannellini beans, haricot beans and pinto beans are best cooked conventionally because they do not cook more quickly in a microwave oven.

To cook conventionally, soak the beans overnight in a large bowl of cold water. The next day, drain, put into a large saucepan and cover with fresh water. Bring to the boil and boil for 10 minutes, then reduce the heat and simmer for 30 minutes–1½ hours or until tender. Drain and use as required.

Certain beans can be cooked more quickly in the microwave oven, if cooking up to 225 g (8 oz). Soak the beans overnight as above, then drain and cover with enough boiling water to come about 2.5 cm (1 inch) above the level of the beans. Cover and cook for the time stated below, stirring occasionally.

Cooked pulses will keep for up to five days in the refrigerator and up to six months in the freezer.

Type of Pulse 225 g (8 oz)	Approximate time on HIGH
Aduki beans	30–35 minutes. Stand for 5 minutes.
Black-eye beans	25–30 minutes. Stand for 5 minutes.
Chickpeas	50–55 minutes. Stand for 5 minutes.
Flageolet beans	40–45 minutes. Stand for 5 minutes.
Mung beans	30–35 minutes. Stand for 5 minutes.

COOKING PASTA, RICE AND GRAINS

Pasta, rice and grains do not cook more quickly in the microwave oven because generally they are dehydrated products needing to be reconstituted before they begin cooking. It is often more sensible use of the microwave to cook these conventionally while making an accompanying sauce in the microwave oven.

Because large quantities of water are slow to heat up in the microwave, it is quicker to boil water in a kettle and then pour over enough to cover the pasta by about 2.5 cm (1 inch).

Rice can be cooked by the absorption method (all the added water is absorbed by the rice during cooking) or by the same method as pasta, adding enough boiling water to cover by about 2.5 cm (1 inch) and then draining after cooking.

There are so many varieties of noodles available that it is impossible to cover the different cooking times. As a general guide they should be cooked in a large bowl with boiling water to cover by about 2.5 cm (1 inch). Cook on HIGH for upwards of 2 minutes or until tender.

Cooking Rice and Grains	Quantity	Approximate time on HIGH
Brown rice	225 g (8 oz)	30–35 minutes
White rice	225 g (8 oz)	12–15 minutes
Basmati rice	225 g (8 oz)	10–12 minutes
Wild rice	100 g (4 oz)	
Millet	225 g (8 oz)	
Buckwheat	225 g (8 oz)	
Wholewheat grains	225 g (8 oz)	25–30 minutes

Put pasta and salt to taste in a large bowl. Pour over enough boiling water to cover the pasta by 2.5 cm (1 inch). Stir, then cover leaving a gap to let steam escape and cook on HIGH for the stated time, stirring occasionally. Leave to stand, covered, for 5 minutes. Do not drain.

Pasta	Quantity	Approximate time on HIGH
Fresh wholemeal/spinach pasta	225 g (8 oz)	3–4 minutes
Dried wholemeal/spinach pasta shapes	175 g (6 oz)	8–10 minutes
Dried wholemeal/spinach pasta shapes	225 g (8 oz)	8–10 minutes
Dried wholemeal/spinach pasta shapes	450 g (1 lb)	12–14 minutes
Dried wholemeal spaghetti	225 g (8 oz)	7–8 minutes
Dried wholemeal spaghetti	450 g (1 lb)	8–10 minutes

UNUSUAL INGREDIENTS AND FLAVOURINGS

Because much of my inspiration for vegetarian eating comes from the cuisines of other countries, many of the ingredients and flavourings used in this book may seem unusual. Thanks to the growing ethnic population and experiences offered by travelling, the shops are now introducing exotic fruits and vegetables, so availability is improving. For example, until recently yams, plantains, star fruit, fresh coriander, okra and limes have only been sold in specialist shops, but they are now stocked by the larger branches of several supermarkets.

Spices, so important in Indian cookery, transform plain vegetables into exotic creations. I'm particularly fond of fresh coriander, ginger and garlic, along with cumin, cloves and cinnamon. They all combine well with strongly flavoured vegetables such as roots, leafy green vegetables and some vegetables that may seem new to us—yams, okra and plantains.

Fresh herbs and good olive or nut oils are perfect flavours for delicate vegetables like mangetouts, courgettes, salad leaves and tomatoes.

Tamarind and lemon grass are favourite Indonesian flavourings. When combined with ginger, garlic and sometimes peanuts, both give a delicious authentic Thai flavour to noodle dishes and soups.

Spices popular in old English cookery, such as ground mixed spice, allspice, cloves and juniper berries, add lively flavour to vegetable pâtés. I've used juniper in the Coarse Herb and Mushroom Pâté on page 46, and in the Green Lentil and Cream Cheese Pâté on page 45, allspice adds richness to the flavour.

Most of the ingredients used in this book can be bought either from a good health food shop or from the appropriate specialist shop. See individual recipe introductions for more information.

HOW TO USE THE RECIPES IN THIS BOOK WITH YOUR COOKER SETTINGS

Unlike conventional ovens, the power output and heat controls on various microwave cookers do not follow a standard formula. When manufacturers refer to a 700-watt cooker, they are referring to the cooker's POWER OUTPUT; its INPUT, which is indicated on the back of the cooker, is double that figure. The higher the wattage of a cooker, the faster the rate of cooking, thus food cooked at 700 watts on full power cooks in half the time of food cooked at 350 watts. That said, the actual cooking performance of one 700-watt cooker may vary slightly from another with the same wattage because factors such as cooker cavity size affect cooking performance. The vast majority of microwave cookers sold today are either 600, 650 or 700 watts, but there are many cookers still in use which may be 400 or 500 watts.

IN THIS BOOK

HIGH refers to 100%/full power output of 600–700 watts.

MEDIUM refers to 60% of full power.

LOW is 35% of full power.

Whatever the wattage of your cooker, the HIGH/FULL setting will always be 100% of the cooker's output. Thus your highest setting will correspond to HIGH.

However, the MEDIUM and LOW settings used in this book may not be equivalent to the MEDIUM and LOW settings marked on your cooker. As these settings vary according to power input, use the following calculation to estimate the correct setting

for a 600–700-watt cooker. This simple calculation should be done before you use the recipes for the first time, to ensure successful results. Multiply the percentage power required by the total number of settings on your cooker and divide by 100. To work out what setting MEDIUM and LOW correspond to on your cooker, use the following calculation

$$Medium\ (60\%)$$
$$= \%\text{Power required}$$
$$\times \text{Total Number}$$
$$\text{of Cooker Settings}$$
$$\div 100 = \text{Correct Setting}$$
$$= \frac{60 \times 9}{100} = 5$$

$$Low\ (35\%)$$
$$= \%\text{Power required}$$
$$\times \text{Total Number}$$
$$\text{of Cooker Settings}$$
$$\div 100 = \text{Correct Setting}$$
$$= \frac{35 \times 9}{100} = 3$$

If your cooker power output is lower than 600 watts, then you must allow a longer cooking and thawing time for all recipes and charts in this book.

Add approximately 10–15 seconds per minute for a 500-watt cooker, and 15–20 seconds per minute for a 400-watt cooker. No matter what the wattage of your cooker is, you should always check food before the end of cooking time, to ensure that it does not get overcooked. Don't forget to allow for standing time.

GENERAL RECIPE NOTES

Follow either metric or imperial measures for the recipes in this book; they are not interchangeable.

Bowl sizes

Small bowl = about 900 ml (1½ pints)
Medium bowl = about 2.3 litres (4 pints)
Large bowl = about 3.4 litres (6 pints)
Large shallow dish = about 30.5 cm (12 inch) diameter

Covering

Cook uncovered unless otherwise stated.
At the time of going to press, it has been recommended by the Ministry of Agriculture, Fisheries and Food that the use of cling film should be avoided in microwave cooking. When a recipe requires you to cover the container, either cover with a lid or a plate, leaving a gap to let steam escape.

Combined oven owners

Combined cookers combine conventional and microwave methods of cooking so that food browns as well as cooking quickly. One of the disadvantages of cooking in a microwave cooker is that baked dishes do not brown or crisp. In this book, we show you how to overcome these disadvantages. If you own a combined cooker you will not have these problems. In this case, follow your manufacturers' instructions.

HOT & COLD SOUPS

Soups are simple, quick and satisfying to make. The soups in this chapter range from sophisticated fruit soups to be served as a refreshing start to a meal or an unusual finale, to something more earthy—a simple selection of vegetables cooked gently in vegetable stock until tender and then puréed to make a smooth, nourishing soup. Follow the methods to devise your own original soups.

All soups can be made in advance and then stored in the refrigerator until required or frozen in portion-size quantities. To serve, pour into a tureen and then reheat on HIGH until the desired temperature is reached, stirring occasionally. Stir in cream or yogurt just before serving. I find that for single people like me or for tired workers, too lazy to cook a meal, they make a wonderful instant hot soup with minimum fuss and washing up. Simply make a batch of soup in advance and then ladle into individual bowls as required. One bowlful takes about 2 minutes on HIGH to heat.

Garnishes add individuality and can transform a visually uninteresting soup into something stunning. A few chopped fresh herbs or a swirl of yogurt is better than nothing, but if you have the time, try a few individual leaves of herbs such as parsley, tarragon or chervil arranged in a pattern floating on the soup or round the edge of the dish. Julienne strips of carrot, pepper or courgette add crunch and colour. Sprinkle grated cheese on to toasted bread cut into shapes and then cook on HIGH for 30 seconds or until the cheese just melts. Serve floating in the soup or as an accompaniment. Toasted nuts, coconut and crisply fried onions add flavour and crunch.

VEGETABLE STOCK

A basic stock to use instead of stock cubes. There is no hard and fast rule about which vegetables to use, but avoid using potatoes as they make the stock cloudy.

► MAKES ABOUT 900 ml ($1\frac{1}{2}$ pints) ◄

2 medium carrots
2 medium onions
3 celery sticks
2 leeks
4 juniper berries
bouquet garni
salt and pepper

1 Finely chop all of the vegetables (including the skins) and put into a large bowl. Pour over 1.1 litres (2 pints) boiling water. Cover and cook on HIGH for 20–30 minutes or until the vegetables are very soft.

2 Strain through a sieve and adjust the seasoning if necessary. Vegetable stock can be stored in the refrigerator for 3–4 days or frozen until required.

HOT & COLD SOUPS

MIXED VEGETABLE SOUP

Make this simple soup when you have lots of vegetables to use up. Use any vegetables at hand but try to include a good mixture for maximum flavour, such as onions, leeks, carrots, parsnips, potatoes, swede, celery, turnip or celeriac— the possibilities are endless. Chop them all finely, to reduce the cooking time. The easiest way to do this is in a food processor. Add a final enrichment of cream or yogurt. Serve with Herb, Cheese and Olive Bread (see page 117).

▶ SERVES 6 ◀

1.1 kg (2½ lb) mixed vegetables (see above)
2 bay leaves
bouquet garni
salt and pepper
150 ml (¼ pint) double cream, crème fraiche, soured cream or single cream (optional)

1 Finely chop the vegetables and put in a large bowl with the bay leaves, bouquet garni and 1.4 litres (2½ pints) water.

2 Cover and cook on HIGH for 30–40 minutes or until the vegetables are very soft. Rub through a sieve or purée in a blender or food processor until smooth.

3 Season to taste with salt and pepper. Return the soup to a clean ovenproof serving bowl and reheat on HIGH for 3–4 minutes or until hot. Stir in cream or yogurt if desired. Serve with Irish Soda Bread (see page 116) for a delicious and nourishing lunch or supper.

HARICOT BEAN AND OLIVE SOUP

This hearty bean and vegetable soup is high in fibre. Serve with garlic bread or Zahter Bread (see page 118) to complement the vegetable protein.

▶ SERVES 6 ◀

30 ml (2 tbsp) olive oil
1 medium onion, skinned and chopped
2 garlic cloves, skinned and crushed
225 g (8 oz) cooked haricot beans (see page 13) or a 425-g (15-oz) can, drained and rinsed
900 ml (1½ pints) vegetable stock (see page 15)
15 ml (1 tbsp) tomato purée
2 celery sticks, trimmed and chopped
100 g (4 oz) green beans cut into 2.5-cm (1-inch) lengths
1 small red pepper, seeded and chopped
1 courgette, sliced
15 ml (1 level tbsp) chopped fresh thyme
50 g (2 oz) stoned black olives, chopped
salt and pepper

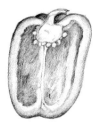

16

1   Put the oil, onion and garlic in a large bowl. Cook on HIGH for 4–5 minutes until softened, stirring occasionally.

2   Add the haricot beans, stock, tomato purée, celery, green beans, pepper, courgette and thyme. Cover and cook on HIGH for 10–12 minutes or until boiling and the vegetables are softened.

3   Stir in the olives, season to taste with salt and pepper and serve hot with garlic or zahter bread.

CORN AND CHICKPEA CHOWDER

Chowders are hearty soups, popular in North America. They usually contain clams or salt pork. Here is a filling, high fibre variation containing the traditional sweetcorn, but with chickpeas instead of meat or fish. Serve with bread to complement the protein.

▶   SERVES 4–6   ◀

1 large onion, skinned
225 g (8 oz) potato, peeled
225 g (8 oz) carrots, scrubbed
2 celery sticks, finely chopped
1 bay leaf
1 strip lemon rind
600 ml (1 pint) vegetable stock (see page 15)
1 egg
450 ml ($\frac{3}{4}$ pint) milk
1 small green pepper, seeded and chopped
225 g (8 oz) cooked chickpeas (see page 13) or a 425-g (15-oz) can, drained and rinsed
198-g (7-oz) can sweetcorn
salt and pepper
30 ml (2 tbsp) chopped fresh parsley

1   Grate the onion, potato and carrot into a large bowl. Add the celery, bay leaf, lemon rind and the stock. Cover and cook on HIGH for 15–20 minutes or until the vegetables are softened.

2   Meanwhile, hard-boil the egg conventionally.

3   Add the milk, green pepper, chickpeas, and sweetcorn to the soup, re-cover and cook on HIGH for 5–6 minutes or until the green pepper is softened and the soup is very hot.

4   Season to taste with salt and pepper and stir in the parsley. Serve garnished with the chopped hard-boiled egg.

Creamy Carrot, Tofu and Caraway Dip, page 27; Mint and Pea Dip, page 28; Aubergine and Pomegranate Dip, page 26, with a selection of crudités

ARTICHOKE SOUP

Delicately-flavoured Jerusalem artichokes are a winter vegetable. They should be used as soon as possible after cutting as they quickly become discoloured. Serve this sophisticated soup as a start to a special meal.

► SERVES 6 ◄

700 g (1½ lb) Jerusalem artichokes, scrubbed and sliced
1 small lemon
25 g (1 oz) butter or margarine
1 medium onion, skinned and chopped
450 ml (¾ pint) milk
30 ml (2 tbsp) chopped fresh parsley
150 ml (¼ pint) single cream
salt and pepper
parsley sprigs, to garnish

1 Put the artichokes in a large bowl. Cut two slices from the lemon and add to the artichokes with the butter or margarine, onion and 450 ml (¾ pint) water.

2 Cover and cook on HIGH for 25–30 minutes or until the artichokes are tender. Discard the lemon slices.

3 Reserve a few slices of artichoke as a garnish, then sieve or purée the remainder in a blender or food processor. Return to the rinsed-out bowl with the milk and the juice from the lemon, re-cover and cook on HIGH for 5–6 minutes or until hot.

4 Stir in the parsley and the cream, and season to taste with salt and pepper. Serve hot, garnished with the reserved artichoke slices cut into shreds, and sprigs of parsley.

SHADES OF GREEN SOUP

This makes a hearty-textured soup to serve on cold wintry days as a light meal. When choosing kale, avoid any with yellow or damaged leaves. It is a delicious green vegetable—a valuable source of vitamins in the winter and a good substitute for cabbage, although it has a much stronger flavour.

► SERVES 4–6 ◄

25 g (1 oz) butter or margarine
450 g (1 lb) kale or spring greens, trimmed and chopped
2 leeks, trimmed and sliced
900 ml (1½ pints) vegetable stock (see page 15)
100 g (4 oz) shelled peas or frozen petit pois
½ cos or Webb's Wonder lettuce, trimmed
salt and pepper
30 ml (2 tbsp) chopped fresh dill
a few toasted almonds, to garnish

1   Put the butter, kale and leeks in a large bowl, cover, and cook on HIGH for 5–7 minutes or until slightly softened, stirring occasionally.

2   Add half of the stock, re-cover and continue to cook on HIGH for 5–10 minutes or until the vegetables are tender.

3   Pass the soup through a sieve or purée in a blender or food processor. Return to the rinsed-out bowl with the remaining stock and the peas. Re-cover and cook on HIGH for 5–7 minutes or until hot.

4   Meanwhile, finely chop the lettuce. Stir the lettuce and dill into the soup. Season to taste and serve sprinkled with toasted almonds.

HOT AND SOUR NOODLE SOUP

This soup includes two common Indonesian flavourings: tamarind and lemon. grass. Tamarind is a dark, curious substance, which is actually the dried fruit of the tamarind tree. It is usually sold in blocks and has a sour flavour. Lemon grass is a species of grass with a delicate lemon flavour due to the presence of citric oils. Both ingredients are available in ethnic grocers. This soup is substantial enough to serve as a main course.

► SERVES 4–6 ◄

50 g (2 oz) tamarind
1 large onion, skinned and sliced
1 green chilli, sliced
1 garlic clove, skinned and crushed
2 bay leaves
15 ml (1 tbsp) vegetable oil
30 ml (2 tbsp) crunchy peanut butter
50 g (2 oz) creamed coconut
50 g (2 oz) thin egg noodles
2 carrots, thinly sliced
half a head of Chinese leaves, coarsely chopped
100 g (4 oz) firm tofu
10 ml (2 tsp) chopped fresh lemon grass or finely grated lemon rind
salt and pepper

1   Put the tamarind in a small bowl and pour over 300 ml ($\frac{1}{2}$ pint) boiling water. Leave to soak while making the soup.

2   Put the onion, chilli, garlic, bay leaves and oil in a large bowl. Cover and cook on HIGH for 4–5 minutes or until the onion is slightly softened.

3   Add the peanut butter, creamed coconut and 600 ml (1 pint) boiling water. Mix well together, then stir in the noodles, the carrots and the cabbage. Re-cover and cook on HIGH for 6–7 minutes until the soup returns to the boil and the noodles are just tender.

4   Strain the tamarind mixture into the soup, discarding the pulp left in the sieve. Cut the tofu into cubes and stir into the soup with the lemon grass or lemon rind. Season to taste. Serve hot.

CREAM OF SAGE SOUP

Onions provide the bulk for this soup, but the predominant flavour is of sage. Do not be tempted to use dried sage as it is a poor substitute for the fresh herb.

► SERVES 4 ◄

25 g (1 oz) butter or margarine
450 g (1 lb) onions, skinned and thinly sliced
600 ml (1 pint) vegetable stock (see page 15)
45 ml (3 tbsp) chopped fresh sage
300 ml ($\frac{1}{2}$ pint) single cream
salt and pepper
fresh sage leaves, to garnish

1 Put the butter or margarine and the onions in a large bowl, cover and cook on HIGH for 7–8 minutes, or until softened.

2 Add the stock and half the sage, re-cover, and cook on HIGH for 10–12 minutes or until very hot and the onions are really soft. Purée in a blender or food processor, then return to the rinsed-out bowl.

3 Stir in the cream and the remaining sage and season to taste with salt and pepper. Reheat on HIGH for 1 minute, if necessary, but do not allow the soup to boil or it will curdle. Serve immediately garnished with sage.

BARLEY SOUP

This chunky soup is a vegetarian version of the famous Scotch broth which contains mutton or beef. This version uses pot barley, rather than the more common pearl barley, because it is less refined and therefore contains more fibre.

► SERVES 6 ◄

25 g (1 oz) pot barley
1.2 litres ($2\frac{1}{4}$ pints) vegetable stock (see page 15)
2 large carrots, chopped
1 medium turnip, peeled and chopped
2 leeks, thinly sliced
1 medium onion, skinned and chopped
bouquet garni
salt and pepper
45 ml (3 level tbsp) chopped fresh parsley

1 Put the barley and half of the stock in a large bowl. Cover and cook on HIGH for 15–20 minutes or until the barley is tender.

2 Add the remaining stock and the carrots, turnip, leeks, onion and the bouquet garni. Re-cover and cook on HIGH for 25–30 minutes or until the vegetables are tender.

3   Remove and discard the bouquet garni and season to taste with salt and pepper. Stir in the parsley and serve immediately with brown rolls.

MARBLED ICED BORTSCH

Bortsch is cooked in various ways all over Eastern Europe. The Polish version is often a clearer soup—to achieve this, strain the soup after completing step 2 and omit the cream in step 4, serving the soup simply topped with a spoonful of soured cream. This method will only serve four people. Puréeing the beetroot makes a thicker soup which turns from dark purple to a pretty pink when the cream is stirred in. Serve the cucumber and dill in small bowls for guests to help themselves and sprinkle on top of their soup if wished.

► SERVES 6 ◄

1 large onion, skinned and chopped
2 carrots, chopped
15 ml (1 tbsp) vegetable oil
450 g (1 lb) cooked beetroot, chopped
1 litre (2 pints) vegetable stock (see page 15)
5 ml (1 level tsp) dark muscovado sugar
15 ml (1 tbsp) lemon juice
salt and pepper
300 ml ($\frac{1}{4}$ pint) soured cream

► *TO SERVE* ◄

$\frac{1}{2}$ a cucumber
30 ml (2 tbsp) chopped fresh dill
pumpernickel bread

1   Put the onion, carrot and oil in a large bowl. Cover and cook on HIGH for 5–6 minutes or until slightly softened.

2   Add the beetroot, stock, sugar and lemon juice, re-cover and cook on HIGH for 10–15 minutes until the beetroot is very soft, stirring occasionally.

3   Push through a sieve or purée in a blender or food processor. Cover and chill for 3–4 hours or overnight.

4   To serve, stir in half of the cream and season to taste with salt and pepper. Pour into a large bowl or individual serving bowls then carefully stir in the remaining cream to make a marbled pattern. Mix the cucumber with the dill, and hand separately. Serve the soup with the cucumber and the pumpernickel bread.

Pear Vichyssoise

Vichyssoise is the classic chilled soup—usually a mixture of leeks and potato, but here fresh pears are included for variety. Make sure that the vegetables are cooked until really soft in step 2 or the velvety smooth texture of the soup will be spoilt.

▶ Serves 4–6 ◀

50 g (2 oz) butter or margarine
2 large leeks, trimmed and thinly sliced
1 onion, skinned and grated
1 large potato, peeled and grated
3 large firm pears, peeled and grated
900 ml (1½ pints) vegetable stock (see page 15)
150 ml (¼ pint) single cream
salt and pepper
fresh chives and chopped pear, to garnish

1   Put the butter or margarine and the leeks and onion in a large bowl, cover and cook on HIGH for 5–7 minutes or until softened, stirring occasionally.

2   Add the potato, pears, and half of the stock, re-cover and cook on HIGH for 10–12 minutes or until the vegetables are really tender, stirring occasionally.

3   Rub through a sieve or purée in a blender or food processor. Add the remaining stock and the cream, then season to taste with salt and pepper. Cover and chill in the refrigerator for at least 4 hours before serving. Serve garnished with chives and chopped pear.

Andalusian Summer Soup

This is a version of the famous Spanish soup called gazpacho. There are numerous variations of this chilled soup throughout Spain, some with lots of tomatoes or lots of cucumber, while some are mostly crushed vegetables with hardly any liquid. This version is typical of southern Spain, in that it is smooth and creamy with a spicy, hot flavour given by the chilli.

▶ Serves 4–6 ◀

30 ml (2 tbsp) olive oil
1 large onion, skinned and chopped
2 garlic cloves, skinned and crushed
2 large red peppers, seeded and chopped
450 g (1 lb) ripe tomatoes, roughly chopped
30 ml (2 tbsp) red wine vinegar
1 dried red chilli, seeded and finely chopped (optional)
salt and pepper
60 ml (4 tbsp) mayonnaise
chopped red or black pepper, chopped fresh parsley, to garnish

1   Put the oil, onion, garlic and peppers in a large bowl. Cover and cook on HIGH for 5–7 minutes until softened, stirring occasionally.

2   Add the tomatoes, vinegar, chilli and 600 ml (1 pint) water. Cover and cook on HIGH for 12–15 minutes or until the vegetables are really soft, stirring occasionally.

3   Season generously with pepper and salt, then pass through a sieve or purée in a blender or food processor. Return to the rinsed-out bowl, cover, and chill in the refrigerator for at least 4 hours before serving.

4   To serve, spoon into individual bowls and top each serving with a spoonful of mayonnaise. Garnish with chopped pepper and parsley. Serve as a starter or light meal with crusty bread.

CHILLED COURGETTE, MINT AND YOGURT SOUP

A light, low-calorie soup, perfect for the weight conscious. Choose tender, young courgettes for the best flavour and do not be tempted to peel them as most of the flavour is in the skin.

▶   SERVES 4–6   ◀

450 g (1 lb) courgettes, trimmed and coarsely grated
1 medium onion, skinned and finely chopped
1 large potato, peeled and grated
600 ml (1 pint) vegetable stock (see page 15)
30 ml (2 tbsp) chopped fresh mint
150 ml ($\frac{1}{4}$ pint) natural yogurt
salt and pepper
courgette slices and sprigs of mint, to garnish

1   Put the onion, potato and half of the stock in a large bowl. Cover and cook on HIGH for 8–10 minutes or until very soft.

2   Add the courgettes and continue to cook on HIGH for 4 minutes or until the courgettes are soft.

3   Pass through a sieve or purée in a blender or food processor. Add the remaining stock, the mint and the yogurt and season to taste with salt and pepper.

4   Cover and chill in the refrigerator for at least 4 hours before serving garnished with courgette slices and mint sprigs.

SPICED CRANBERRY SOUP

*Cranberries have a very short season but are available frozen throughout the year.
For maximum effect, serve this soup in large, stemmed wine glasses or glass
bowls as a starter or as a dessert (see the photograph facing page 16).*

▶ SERVES 4 ◀

350 g (12 oz) cranberries
4 whole cloves
1 cinnamon stick
45 ml (3 tbsp) runny honey
15 ml (1 tbsp) Crème de Cassis
a few cranberries, mint leaves, to decorate

1   Put the cranberries, cloves, cinnamon, and honey in a large bowl with
600 ml (1 pint) water. Cover and cook on HIGH for 10–12 minutes or
until the cranberries are tender.

2   Cool slightly then pass the soup through a sieve to remove the skins.
Stir in the Crème de Cassis. Cover and chill in the refrigerator for at least
4 hours before serving.

3   To serve, spoon the soup into individual bowls and decorate each
with a few cranberries and mint leaves.

TART APPLE AND GINGER SOUP

*This unusual soup makes a refreshing start to any meal. Fresh ginger has the
best flavour and should be used in preference to ground. Here both are used to
emphasise the flavour.*

▶ SERVES 4 ◀

25 g (1 oz) butter or margarine
2.5-cm (1-inch) piece fresh root ginger, peeled and grated
large pinch of ground ginger
1 large cooking apple
600 ml (1 pint) vegetable stock (see page 15)
salt and pepper
chopped red apple, to garnish

1   Put the butter, fresh ginger and ground ginger in a large bowl and
cook on HIGH for 2 minutes, stirring once.

2   Chop the apples roughly (including the peel and core) and add to the
ginger with the stock. Cover and cook on HIGH for 10–15 minutes or
until the apple is very soft.

3   Pass the soup through a sieve into a clean bowl and season to taste
with salt and pepper. Cover and chill in the refrigerator for at least 4 hours
before serving, garnished with red apple.

DIPS & SAUCES

When is a dip not a dip? When it's thinned down to make a sauce. The dips in this chapter are all suitable as a starter or a snack or nibble at any time of day, but thinned down with a little cream, yogurt or silken tofu they can be transformed into sauces for serving with lightly cooked vegetables or pasta, noodles, rice, beans or terrines.

I love serving an assortment of dips with a selection of raw vegetable or fruit crudités chosen and prepared to appeal to the eye. Baby vegetables such as carrots look good with a little green top left attached. Cut vegetables into neat strips all about the same size and arrange in tidy rows of colour, or go for the wild approach (see the photograph facing page 1/), merely trimming vegetables to a manageable size but retaining much of the original shape, and arrange in a more chaotic fashion.

Sliced fresh fruit such as apples, pears, nectarines and fresh dates as well as dried figs, dates and apricots all make nutritious and unusual crudités.

RADICCHIO AND ALMOND DIP

Soaking radicchio in a bowl of cold water helps to eliminate some of the bitter taste and makes it crisp and fresh. Once softened in a little oil the red lettuce can be puréed to make an interesting dip. Serve with grissini (bread sticks) before a main course of pasta for a thoroughly Italian meal.

▶ SERVES 4–6 ◀

2 large heads of radicchio
15 ml (1 tbsp) almond or walnut oil
200 ml (7 fl oz) double cream
75 ml (5 level tbsp) ground almonds
salt and pepper
radicchio leaves, to serve

1   Immerse the radicchio in a large bowl of cold water and leave to soak for 2–3 hours. Drain the radicchio then remove the tough central core and discard. Chop roughly.

2   Put the oil in a large bowl and cook on HIGH for 30 seconds or until hot. Stir in the radicchio and cook on HIGH for 2 minutes or until just wilted, stirring occasionally.

3   Put in a blender or food processor with the cream and almonds and purée until smooth. Season to taste with salt. Leave to cool. Chill and then serve in a bowl lined with radicchio leaves.

AUBERGINE AND POMEGRANATE DIP

Aubergines are so easy to cook whole in the microwave, and they retain all their flavour and vitamins. Once you have discovered this method of cooking them, you will never return to the arduous conventional methods of baking or grilling. Cooking in the microwave also means that the dark aubergine skin is soft enough to be included in purées, adding colour, texture and flavour.

▶ SERVES 4–6 ◀

1 large aubergine weighing about 450 g (1 lb)
1 garlic clove, skinned and crushed
30 ml (2 tbsp) olive oil
1 large ripe pomegranate
150 ml ($\frac{1}{4}$ pint) natural yogurt
salt and pepper

1 Prick the aubergine all over with a fork, then place in the oven and cook on HIGH for 6–10 minutes, or until the aubergine feels soft when squeezed gently, turning over once during cooking.

2 Leave to cool slightly, then cut off the stalk and discard it. Put the aubergine, garlic and the oil in a blender or food processor and purée until smooth. Leave to cool.

3 Meanwhile, cut the pomegranate in half and scoop the seeds out into a sieve. Hold the sieve over the bowl of the blender or food processor and push on the seeds to extract the juice. Reserve the seeds to garnish.

4 When the aubergine is cool, add the yogurt and season to taste with salt and pepper. Purée until well mixed. Leave until cold.

5 Serve cold, decorated with the reserved pomegranate seeds, with warm pitta bread or a selection of vegetable and fruit crudités.

CABBAGE AND SESAME DIP

Buy a large bright green cabbage with the outside leaves intact. The heart of the cabbage is cut away and the outer shell left to make the perfect receptacle for serving the dip. Serve with warmed pitta bread, cut into strips for dunking.

▶ SERVES 4–6 ◀

50 g (2 oz) sesame seeds
1 large savoy cabbage
150 ml ($\frac{1}{4}$ pint) milk
1 bay leaf
30 ml (2 tbsp) tahini
30 ml (2 tbsp) runny honey
75 ml (5 tbsp) single cream
15 ml (1 tbsp) lemon juice
salt and pepper

1   Spread the sesame seeds out on a large flat plate and cook on HIGH for 8–9 minutes or until lightly toasted, stirring occasionally. Reserve a few to garnish, then put the remainder in a blender or food processor with 30 ml (2 tbsp) water and purée until smooth.

2   Meanwhile, using a sharp serrated knife cut out the centre of the cabbage, leaving the base and outside leaves intact. This makes a container for the dip.

3   Roughly chop the scooped-out cabbage and put into a large bowl with the milk, the bay leaf, and the sesame seeds.

4   Cover and cook on HIGH for 6–8 minutes or until the cabbage is really tender. Put into the blender or food processor with the tahini, honey, cream, lemon juice and salt and pepper to taste and purée until smooth. Leave to cool then chill before serving.

5   To serve, wash the cabbage shell thoroughly to remove any dirt then cook with just the water clinging to the leaves on HIGH for 1–2 minutes or just until it turns bright green. Rinse immediately in cold water and drain. Spoon the cabbage and tahini dip into the centre. Sprinkle with the reserved sesame seeds and serve immediately with fresh crudités.

CREAMY CARROT, TOFU AND CARAWAY DIP

Tofu is bland in flavour but high in protein. It has a smooth, creamy texture when whizzed in a blender, making it the perfect vehicle for dips and sauces. Carrots and caraway make an unusual dip, perfect for serving with chunks of wholemeal or granary bread. This dip may also be thinned to a pouring consistency with a little natural yogurt or vegetable stock to serve as a sauce with cooked vegetables or Grated Cheese and Vegetable Terrine (page 52).

▶   SERVES 6   ◀

15 ml (1 level tbsp) caraway seeds
5 ml (1 level tsp) dried dill weed
15 ml (1 tbsp) vegetable oil
450 g (1 lb) carrots, thinly sliced
1 small onion, skinned and finely chopped
275 g (10 oz) silken tofu
salt and pepper
grated carrot, to garnish

1   Lightly crush the caraway seeds and put into a large bowl with the dill and the vegetable oil. Cook on HIGH for 2 minutes, stirring once.

2   Add the carrots, onion and 30 ml (2 tbsp) water. Cover and cook on HIGH for 10–12 minutes or until the vegetables are tender, stirring once.

3   When the vegetables are cool, put into a blender or food processor and purée until smooth. Add the tofu and mix thoroughly together. Season to taste with salt and pepper. Garnish with grated carrot.

MINT AND PEA DIP

Unless you grow your own or live in an area with a farm where you can pick your own, you will probably be more familiar with ready-shelled frozen peas than you are with fresh peas in the pod. Although there is something satisfying about shelling peas, it is not a fast process and perhaps not attractive to the time-conscious microwave user. So here frozen peas are used for reasons of convenience and speed, with no sacrifice of flavour or vitamins. Serve chilled, garnished generously with sprigs of mint with a selection of whole baby vegetables such as new carrots, mangetouts and baby radishes for dipping.

▶ SERVES 6 ◀

25 g (1 oz) butter or margarine
450 g (1 lb) frozen peas
150 ml ($\frac{1}{4}$ pint) vegetable stock
3 spring onions, trimmed and chopped
1 small green lettuce, shredded
5 ml (1 level tsp) light muscovado sugar
45 ml (3 tbsp) chopped fresh mint
salt and pepper
mint sprigs, to garnish

1 Put the butter, peas, stock and onions in a medium bowl. Cover and cook on HIGH for 5–7 minutes or until the peas are tender. Reserve a few to garnish.

2 Stir in the lettuce and the sugar and cook on HIGH for 1–2 minutes or until the lettuce is just wilted.

3 Purée in a blender or food processor, then stir in the mint. Season to taste, and then chill before serving. Serve garnished with the reserved peas and mint sprigs.

PEAR AND LEEK SAUCE

The combination of pears and leeks is most successful, producing a well-flavoured sauce, and few can identify the ingredients. The butter or margarine is added for extra richness, but if you wish to reduce calories, omit the fat and add a little extra vegetable stock. Serve with vegetable or nut terrines (see pages 49–52) or pour over mixed cooked vegetables of your choice.

▶ MAKES ABOUT 450 ml ($\frac{3}{4}$ pint) ◀

460 g (1 lb) hard pears
450 g (1 lb) leeks
1 garlic clove, skinned and crushed
150 ml ($\frac{1}{4}$ pint) vegetable stock (see page 15)
10 ml (2 level tsp) light muscovado sugar
50 g (2 oz) butter or margarine
salt and pepper

1   Peel, core and roughly chop the pears. Trim and thinly slice the leeks. Put the pears, leeks, garlic, stock and sugar in a large bowl. Cover and cook on HIGH for 12–14 minutes or until really soft.

2   Put the sauce in a blender or food processor with the butter and purée until smooth. Season to taste with salt and pepper. Serve hot.

CREAM AND MUSHROOM SAUCE

Use this creamy sauce to liven up plainly cooked vegetables, or serve with hot Stuffed Vegetables (see page 74), a vegetable terrine (see pages 49–52), or tossed with freshly cooked pasta. Use soured or single cream if you wish to reduce the calories, in which case do not allow the sauce to boil or it will curdle.

▶ MAKES ABOUT 300 ml ($\frac{1}{2}$ pint) ◀

15 g ($\frac{1}{2}$ oz) butter or margarine
100 g (4 oz) button mushrooms, sliced
1 garlic clove, skinned and crushed (optional)
45 ml (3 tbsp) dry white wine or vegetable stock (see page 15)
150 ml ($\frac{1}{4}$ pint) double cream
salt and pepper

1   Put the butter or margarine, mushrooms and garlic into a medium bowl and cook on HIGH for 2–3 minutes or until the mushrooms are softened.

2   Add the wine or stock and cook for 2 minutes or until boiling.

3   Add the cream and season generously with black pepper and a little salt. Cook on HIGH for 3 minutes or until slightly reduced, stirring occasionally. Serve hot.

SMOOTH GREEN SAUCE

*This makes a delicate green spinach sauce with added protein in the form of tofu.
If you grow sorrel or Good King Henry in your garden use that in place of the
spinach. Add a little cheese such as ricotta, Parmesan or blue cheese for extra
flavour. Serve with pasta or cooked beans or grains of your choice.*

▶ MAKES ABOUT 450 ml (¾ pint) ◀

15 ml (1 tbsp) vegetable oil
1 garlic clove, skinned and crushed
1 small onion, skinned and chopped
450 g (1 lb) fresh spinach, washed, trimmed and chopped, or a 226-g (8-oz) packet frozen spinach
100 g (4 oz) silken tofu
freshly grated nutmeg
salt and pepper

1 Put the oil, garlic and onion in a medium bowl. Cover and cook on
HIGH for 3–4 minutes or until softened.

2 Stir in the spinach. If using fresh, cover and cook on HIGH for
3–4 minutes or until the spinach is just cooked. If using frozen spinach,
cook on HIGH for 8–9 minutes or until thawed. Drain.

3 Put the spinach in a blender or food processor and chop roughly. Add
the tofu and purée until smooth. Season generously with nutmeg and salt
and pepper.

4 Return to the bowl and cook on HIGH for 2–3 minutes or until hot.
Serve with pasta or cooked beans of your choice.

ROASTED NUT AND CREAM SAUCE

*Once discovered, the technique of roasting nuts in the microwave should not be
forgotten, but used at every opportunity to brown nuts for incorporating into
pilaffs, salads or stews. This sauce is perfect tossed with spinach pasta or baby
new potatoes cooked in their skins. To make an intriguing sweet sauce to serve
instead of cream or custard, use a sweet wine, omit the seasonings, using a little
ground cinnamon instead, and sweeten with 15–30 ml (1–2 tbsp) runny honey
in step 3.*

▶ MAKES ABOUT 300 ml (½ pint) ◀

100 g (4 oz) hazelnuts, almonds, walnuts, cashew nuts or pecan nuts
150 ml (¼ pint) dry white wine or vegetable stock (see page 15)
150 ml (¼ pint) double cream or Greek strained yogurt
ground mace
salt and pepper

1 Spread the nuts out on a large plate and cook on HIGH for 4–5 minutes until lightly browned. If using hazelnuts tip the nuts on to a clean teatowel and rub off the loose brown skin. Chop finely.

2 Put the wine or stock in a medium bowl and cook on HIGH for 3–4 minutes until boiling. If using wine, cook for a further 2 minutes. Add the nuts and the cream and season to taste with ground mace and salt and pepper.

3 Cook on HIGH for 3–4 minutes until boiling and slightly reduced. Serve hot or warm.

TOMATO SAUCE

This sauce has endless variations and uses; make it in the summer with fresh tomatoes when they are red and plentiful, adding a little tomato purée for extra colour and flavour. Add chopped black or green olives, capers, pinenuts, dried fruit or lightly cooked chopped vegetables to suit your taste. Serve hot with Grated Cheese and Vegetable Terrine (see page 52) or Herby Aubergine and Cheese Terrine (see page 50) or with pasta, or cold with nut burgers.

▶ MAKES ABOUT 600 ml (1 pint) ◀

75 ml (1 tbsp) olive oil
1 large onion, skinned and finely chopped
1 celery stick, finely chopped
1 carrot, finely chopped
1 garlic clove, skinned and crushed (optional)
397-g (14-oz) can tomatoes
10 ml (2 tsp) tomato purée
5 ml (1 level tsp) light muscovado sugar
150 ml ($\frac{1}{4}$ pint) vegetable stock
45 ml (3 tbsp) chopped fresh mixed herbs (optional)
salt and pepper

1 Put the oil, onion, celery, carrot and garlic, if using, in a large bowl. Cover and cook on HIGH for 5–7 minutes or until very soft, stirring occasionally.

2 Add the tomatoes with their juice, tomato purée, sugar and the vegetable stock and cook on HIGH for 10 minutes or until the sauce has reduced and thickened, stirring occasionally.

3 Stir in the herbs and season to taste with salt and pepper. For a smooth sauce, purée in a blender or food processor, then return to the rinsed-out bowl or a serving jug. Cook on HIGH for 2 minutes or until hot.

HARISSA SAUCE

This is a fiery hot sauce, usually served with Couscous (see page 84). Serve with rice or mixed bean dishes, for those who like their food hot.

► MAKES ABOUT 300 ml (½ pint) ◄

15 ml (1 tbsp) vegetable oil
1 large red pepper, seeded and chopped
2 red chillies, seeded and chopped
2 garlic cloves, skinned and crushed
15 ml (1 level tbsp) ground coriander
5 ml (1 level tsp) ground caraway
salt and pepper

1 Put all the ingredients in a medium bowl and mix well together. Cover and cook on HIGH for 8–10 minutes or until the pepper is really soft.

2 Add 300 ml (½ pint) water, re-cover and cook on HIGH for 3–4 minutes or until the water is boiling.

3 Push through a sieve or purée in a blender or food processor until smooth. Season to taste with salt and pepper. Reheat on HIGH for 2–3 minutes or serve cold.

HAZELNUT AND CORIANDER PESTO

This makes a vibrant green pesto with a pungent smell and a strong flavour. Serve it separately for guests to mix to taste with their individual plates of steaming pasta, dilute it with yogurt and toss with cooked vegetables, or use in small amounts to flavour vinaigrette dressings for hot or cold salads.

► MAKES ABOUT 300 ml (½ pint) (ENOUGH FOR 4–6 SERVINGS OF PASTA) ◄

75 g (3 oz) hazelnuts
1 large bunch of coriander weighing about 100 g (4 oz)
2–3 garlic cloves, skinned and crushed
finely grated rind and juice of half a lemon
about 150 ml (¼ pint) olive, sunflower or corn oil
salt and pepper

1 Spread the hazelnuts out on a large plate and cook on HIGH for 4–5 minutes or until lightly toasted. Tip into a blender or food processor.

2 Trim the stalks from the coriander and discard. Put the leaves into the blender with the garlic and the lemon rind and juice. Process until finely chopped, then with the machine still running, gradually add the oil in a thin, steady stream until you have a fairly thick sauce-like consistency.

3 Season with black pepper and a little salt. Turn into a bowl or a jar, cover tightly, and use as required. Store in the refrigerator for 1–2 weeks.

Individual Pastry Tarts with Three Fillings, page 36

SAVOURIES & SNACKS

Convenience foods are usually overprocessed and contain large amounts of fat, sugar and salt and possibly harmful additives. With a microwave cooker the problem of making healthy food fast, is solved. Baked potatoes can be cooked in a fraction of the time it would normally take, ready for stuffing with a filling of your choice.

Scrambled eggs make a good snack. When made in the microwave they are light and fluffy and never stick to the cooking container (see recipe for Scrambled Eggs en Brioche) so there are no dirty pans to clean. Eggs en cocotte are easy too—to serve one, simply break an egg into a ramekin dish and gently prick the yolk with a fine skewer. Cook on MEDIUM for 1–1½ minutes or until the white is just set. Top with a spoonful of double cream then cook on MEDIUM for a further 30 seconds. Leave to stand for 2 minutes, then it is ready to eat. Another good quick snack is Gruyère bread—slice a small French loaf as if making garlic bread, then lightly butter the cut sides and fill with thin slices of Gruyère cheese. Wrap in greaseproof paper and cook on HIGH for one minute or until the cheese just melts. I can never resist eating these immediately they come out of the oven! This chapter also contains recipes for pizza, burgers and spicy nuts, all quick, easy-to-make snacks. Other recipes are suitable as snacks or to eat as part of or as a start to a main meal.

ROSEMARY NUTS

A tasty and satisfying alternative to bought peanut and crisp snacks. Use other fresh herbs if you prefer. Store in an airtight container and nibble as a snack or sprinkle over vegetable stews to add crunch and protein.

▶ SERVES 4–6 ◀

45 ml (3 tbsp) walnut oil
15 ml (1 level tbsp) sweet paprika
350 g (12 oz) walnut halves
30 ml (2 level tbsp) chopped fresh rosemary or 15 ml (1 level tbsp) dried rosemary
salt (optional)

1 Put the oil and paprika in a browning dish and cook on HIGH for 1–1½ minutes until the oil is hot, stirring occasionally.

2 Add the walnuts and the rosemary and toss to coat in the oil. Cook on HIGH for 2–3 minutes until hot, stirring occasionally.

3 Drain on a double sheet of kitchen paper to absorb any excess oil and sprinkle with salt, if liked. Serve warm or cold. Store in an airtight container for 1–2 weeks.

33

Bean and Rice Burgers with Fresh Mango Chutney, page 38

SPICY NUT KOFTAS WITH RAITA

Have these spicy nut balls as a snack or as a starter before an Indian-style meal.
Raita is an Indian speciality made of yogurt usually flavoured with mint or
cucumber. I like to flavour it with other herbs such as coriander with a little
ground cinnamon or cumin and serve it with a variety of dishes including baked
potatoes or spooned on top of bean stews.

▶ SERVES 4 ◀

15 ml (1 tbsp) vegetable oil
1 medium onion, skinned and finely chopped
2 medium carrots, finely grated
1 garlic clove, skinned and crushed
10 ml (2 level tsp) ground coriander
10 ml (2 level tsp) ground cumin
5 ml (1 level tsp) ground fenugreek
5 ml (1 level tsp) ground cardamom
225 g (8 oz) chopped mixed nuts
100 g (4 oz) fresh brown breadcrumbs
salt and pepper
1 egg

▶ *FOR THE RAITA* ◀

300 ml ($\frac{1}{2}$ pint) natural yogurt
half a cucumber, finely chopped
30 ml (2 tbsp) lemon juice
5 ml (1 level tsp) ground cinnamon, or chopped fresh mint or chopped fresh coriander to taste

1 Put the oil, onion, carrots and garlic in a large bowl. Cover and cook on HIGH for 5–7 minutes or until the vegetables are soft, stirring occasionally.

2 Stir in the coriander, cumin, fenugreek and cardamom and cook on HIGH for 1 minute.

3 Add the nuts and breadcrumbs and season to taste with salt and pepper. Mix thoroughly together, then add enough egg to bind.

4 Shape the mixture into 16 balls and arrange in a circle on a baking sheet or a large plate.

5 To make the raita, mix the cucumber, lemon juice and cinnamon, mint or coriander together and season to taste with salt and pepper.

6 Cook the koftas on HIGH for 2–3 minutes or until hot and firm to the touch. Serve hot with the raita, or alone, in pitta bread with salad.

VEGETARIAN SATAY

Satay is an Indonesian speciality consisting of marinated chicken or beef served with a spicy peanut sauce. Here is a vegetarian alternative, using tofu. The success of this dish depends on the thorough marinating of the tofu, so do marinate it overnight if possible. Serve this as a starter or light meal with chunks of cucumber and rice cakes.

▶ SERVES 4–6 ◀

▶ *FOR THE MARINADE* ◀

2 garlic cloves, skinned and crushed
2.5-cm (1-inch) piece fresh root ginger, peeled and finely grated
45 ml (3 tbsp) soy sauce
30 ml (2 tbsp) vegetable oil
10 ml (2 level tsp) dark muscovado sugar
550 g (1 lb 4 oz) firm tofu

▶ *FOR THE SATAY SAUCE* ◀

1 small onion, skinned and finely chopped
15 ml (1 tbsp) vegetable oil
5 ml (1 level tsp) chilli powder
5 ml (1 level tsp) chopped fresh lemon grass or finely grated lemon rind
1 garlic clove, skinned and crushed
50 g (2 oz) creamed coconut
60 ml (4 tbsp) crunchy peanut butter
30 ml (2 tbsp) soy sauce

1   To make the marinade, mix the garlic, ginger, soy sauce, oil and sugar together in a large shallow dish.

2   Cut the tofu into small cubes and add to the marinade, cover and leave in the fridge for at least 2–3 hours, or overnight, stirring occasionally.

3   Meanwhile, make the satay sauce. Put the onion in a browning dish with the oil and cook on HIGH for 7–10 minutes or until well browned, stirring occasionally.

4   Add the chilli powder, lemon grass, garlic, coconut, peanut butter, soy sauce and 150 ml ($\frac{1}{4}$ pint) boiling water. Stir thoroughly to mix, then cook on HIGH for 3–4 minutes until boiling. Spoon into a bowl and set aside.

5   Thread the tofu on to 12 bamboo skewers and arrange in a single layer in the dish containing the marinade. Cook on MEDIUM for 8–10 minutes, or until hot, basting frequently and turning during cooking.

6   Serve the tofu hot with the satay sauce handed separately.

Individual Pastry Tarts with Three Fillings

These light, crisp pastry tarts can be filled with one of the fillings suggested below or a filling of your own choosing. Serve as an attractive starter or with a side salad as a light lunch dish (see the photograph facing page 32).

▶ **Makes 4** ◀

▶ *FOR THE PASTRY* ◀

100 g (4 oz) plain wholemeal flour
salt
50 g (2 oz) butter or margarine
45 ml (3 tbsp) chopped fresh mixed herbs

1 To make the pastry, put the flour and salt to taste in a bowl. Add the butter or margarine and rub in until the mixture resembles fine breadcrumbs. Add 30–60 ml (2–4 tbsp) water and mix together using a round-bladed knife. Knead lightly to give a firm, smooth dough.

2 Roll out the dough thinly. Invert four 10-cm (4-inch) shallow glass flan dishes and cover the bases and sides with the dough. Cover and chill while making the filling.

Brie and Watercress Filling

25 g (1 oz) butter or margarine
2 bunches watercress
275 g (10 oz) ripe Brie
45 ml (3 tbsp) double cream
freshly grated nutmeg
salt and pepper

Put the butter or margarine in a medium bowl and cook on HIGH for 1 minute or until melted. Trim and discard the tough stalks from the watercress. Reserve a few sprigs to garnish and stir the remainder into the butter. Cook on HIGH for 1–2 minutes until just wilted. Remove the rind from the cheese and cut into small pieces. Stir into the watercress with the cream. Cook on HIGH for 1–2 minutes until melted. Season to taste with nutmeg, salt and pepper.

Puréed Mangetout Filling

450 g (1 lb) mangetout, topped and tailed
150 ml ($\frac{1}{4}$ pint) soured cream
salt and pepper

Put the mangetouts and 30 ml (2 tbsp) water in a large bowl. Cover and cook on HIGH for 2 minutes, remove a few mangetouts and reserve for the garnish then continue to cook the remainder on HIGH for 5–6 minutes or until the mangetouts are really tender, stirring occasionally. Cool slightly, then purée in a blender or food processor with the cream. Season to taste with salt and pepper.

Creamy Leek and Parmesan Filling

700 g (1½ lb) leeks, finely sliced
25 g (1 oz) butter or margarine
60 ml (4 tbsp) freshly grated Parmesan cheese
150 ml (¼ pint) double cream
salt and pepper

Reserve a few of the green slices of leek for the garnish then put the remainder and the butter or margarine in a medium bowl. Cover and cook on HIGH for 8–10 minutes until really soft, stirring occasionally. Add the remaining ingredients and cook on HIGH for 1–2 minutes until hot.

1   To cook the tarts, uncover and prick all over with a fork. Arrange pastry side uppermost in a circle in the oven and cook on HIGH for 2–3 minutes or until firm to the touch.

2   Leave to stand for 5 minutes then carefully loosen around the edge and invert on to a large serving plate.

3   Fill with your chosen filling and cook on HIGH for 2–3 minutes or until warmed through. Garnish appropriately.

CREAMY SCRAMBLED EGGS EN BRIOCHE

Scrambled eggs are a delight to make in the microwave as they never stick to the bowl, no messy pans to wash up, and they always appear from the oven light and fluffy. It is important to stir frequently as in conventional cooking or the heat of the bowl will make the eggs set into a hard ring around the edge.

▶   SERVES 2   ◀

2 individual size brioches
4 eggs
60 ml (4 tbsp) double cream or milk
25–50 g (1–2 oz) butter or margarine
salt and pepper
chopped fresh tarragon, chervil, parsley or chives (optional)
a few watercress or salad leaves, to garnish

1   Cut the tops off of the brioches and scoop out the crumbs from the bottom halves to make a container. Discard the crumbs.

2   Put the eggs, cream, butter and salt and pepper to taste in a medium bowl and whisk together.

3   Cook on HIGH for 3–4 minutes or until the eggs are very lightly scrambled, stirring frequently. Stir in the herbs, if using, then leave to stand while warming the brioches.

4   Wrap the brioches loosely in kitchen paper and cook on HIGH for 30 seconds–1 minute or until just hot. Spoon the scrambled eggs into the warmed brioches and replace the lids at an angle. Serve immediately.

Bean and Rice Burgers with Fresh Mango Chutney

These tasty vegetarian burgers can be made in advance and reheated before serving. Make sure that you mash the beans thoroughly in step 3 or the mixture will not hold together. To make burgers suitable for vegans, omit the egg and beat the mixture for longer, the burgers will not be as firm but they will hold their shape. See the photograph facing page 33.

▶ SERVES 4 ◀

100 g (4 oz) brown rice
225 g (8 oz) cooked beans such as red kidney, black-eye, aduki (see page 13), or a 425-g (14-oz) can, drained and rinsed
1–2 garlic cloves, skinned and crushed
2.5 ml ($\frac{1}{2}$ tsp) curry paste
10 ml (2 tsp) tomato purée
1-cm ($\frac{1}{2}$-inch) piece fresh root ginger, peeled and grated
salt and pepper
1 small egg
50 g (2 oz) medium oatmeal

▶ FOR THE MANGO CHUTNEY ◀

1 ripe mango
30 ml (2 tbsp) shredded coconut
finely grated rind and juice of 1 lime

1 Put the rice in a medium bowl and pour over enough boiling water to cover by about 5 cm (2 inches). Cover and cook on HIGH for 20–25 minutes or until tender.

2 Meanwhile, make the mango chutney. Peel the mango and discard the stone. Cut the flesh into small pieces and mix with the remaining ingredients. Leave to stand while making the burgers.

3 When the rice is cooked, drain and leave to cool slightly. Put the beans into a bowl and mash thoroughly with a potato masher or a fork. Add the garlic, curry paste, tomato purée, ginger and the rice. Season to taste with salt and pepper and beat thoroughly until the mixture just begins to cling together.

4 Add enough egg to bind the mixture together, then shape into 8 burgers. Spread the oatmeal out on a plate and press the burgers into it to coat lightly.

5 Arrange in a circle on a baking sheet or the turntable and cook on HIGH for 2 minutes. Turn over and cook on HIGH for a further 2 minutes or until firm to the touch.

6 Serve hot with the mango chutney and a mixed salad or put into pitta bread or wholemeal rolls.

PIZZA WITH CAPERS AND PINENUTS

Use this basic pizza method to experiment with toppings of your choice. If your cooker has a plain white turntable, it can be removed with the cooked pizza on it and used as the perfect pizza serving plate!

▶ SERVES 4–6 ◀

▶ *FOR THE TOPPING* ◀

400-g (14-oz) can chopped tomatoes
1 garlic clove, skinned and crushed
15 ml (1 tbsp) tomato purée
15 ml (1 tbsp) chopped fresh oregano or 5 ml (1 level tsp) dried
salt and pepper
100 g (4 oz) mushrooms, thinly sliced
a few black olives
a few pinenuts
a few capers
100 g (4 oz) mozzarella cheese
fresh oregano
15 ml (1 tbsp) olive oil

▶ *FOR THE PIZZA BASE* ◀

225 g (8 oz) plain wholemeal flour
salt
50 g (2 oz) butter or margarine
150 ml ($\frac{1}{4}$ pint) milk

1   To make the topping, put the tomatoes, garlic, tomato purée and oregano in a bowl and cook on HIGH for 8–10 minutes, or until thickened and reduced. Season to taste with salt and pepper.

2   Meanwhile, make the base. Put the flour and salt to taste in a bowl, then rub in the butter or margarine until the mixture resembles fine breadcrumbs. Add the milk and mix to a soft dough.

3   Thoroughly grease the microwave turntable or a baking sheet. Roll out the dough on a lightly floured surface and place on the turntable or baking sheet. Cook on HIGH for 4–6 minutes or until slightly risen and firm to the touch.

4   Spread the tomato mixture on top of the base and sprinkle with the mushrooms, olives, pinenuts and capers. Cut the cheese into very thin slices and arrange on top. Sprinkle with oregano and drizzle with the olive oil and season generously with pepper.

5   Cook on HIGH for 3–4 minutes or until the topping is hot and the cheese has melted. Serve cut into wedges with salad.

BAKED POTATOES AND FILLINGS

Microwave baked potatoes are the perfect meal in a hurry, providing hot and filling high-fibre food in minutes. They are delicious topped simply with grated cheese, a dollop of natural yogurt and a generous seasoning of black pepper or fresh herbs such as chives or coriander, or piled high with one of the fillings suggested below.

▶ SERVES 4 ◀

4 large potatoes, each weighing about 175 g (6 oz)

Avocado and Smoked Cheese Filling

2 large ripe avocados

150 ml ($\frac{1}{4}$ pint) Greek yogurt

lemon juice

100 g (4 oz) smoked hard cheese

salt and pepper

Cut one of the avocados in half and scoop out the flesh. Mash with a fork or purée in a blender or processor with the yogurt and lemon juice to taste. Peel the remaining avocado and cut into cubes. Cut the cheese into cubes. Fold the cheese and avocado into the puréed ingredients and season to taste with salt and pepper. Use to fill the potatoes as below.

Hot Chilli Bean Filling

397-g (14-oz) can chopped tomatoes

10 ml (2 tsp) tomato purée

2 garlic cloves, skinned and crushed

2.5 ml ($\frac{1}{2}$ level tsp) chilli powder

2.5 ml ($\frac{1}{2}$ level tsp) dried oregano

225 g (8 oz) cooked red kidney beans (see page 13) or a 425-g (14-oz) can red kidney beans, drained and rinsed

30 ml (2 tbsp) chopped fresh coriander or parsley (optional)

salt and pepper

Put all of the ingredients into a large bowl and cook uncovered on HIGH for 10 minutes or until reduced and thickened. Use to fill the potatoes as below.

Carrot, Peanut and Alfalfa Filling

75 ml (5 tbsp) natural yogurt

45 ml (3 tbsp) peanut butter

45 ml (3 tbsp) mayonnaise

4 large carrots, coarsely grated

75 g (3 oz) salted peanuts

75 g (3 oz) alfalfa

squeeze of lemon juice

black pepper

Beat the yogurt, peanut butter and mayonnaise together, then gradually fold in the carrots, peanuts and alfalfa. Season to taste with lemon juice and black pepper. Use to fill the potatoes as below.

1   If using the Chilli Bean filling, make it before cooking the potatoes and set aside. Wash and scrub the potatoes and prick all over with a fork. Arrange in the oven in a circle.

2   Cook on HIGH for 12–14 minutes, or until the potatoes feel soft when gently squeezed, turning them over once during cooking.

3   While the potatoes are cooking make the Avocado and Smoked Cheese, or the Carrot, Peanut and Alfalfa Filling.

4   When the potatoes are cooked, cut them in half and mash the flesh lightly with a fork. Pile your chosen filling on top and serve immediately.

MELTED CHEESE, RADICCHIO AND MANGO SANDWICH

This simple sandwich for two makes brilliant use of the microwave—allowing it to melt the cheese to perfection while just warming the bread and mango in less than 2 minutes. The combination of mango, cheese and radicchio is a new variation on the sweet and sour theme—the mango counteracting the slight bitterness of the radicchio. Experiment with variations for yourself, following the basic method; try mozzarella cheese, tomato and fresh basil, or Gruyère cheese and thinly sliced fresh pear. Serve as a snack, or begin with Pear Vichyssoise (see page 22) for a light lunch or supper dish.

▶   SERVES 2   ◀

1 small ripe mango
100 g (4 oz) mozzarella, Camembert or Cheddar cheese, thinly sliced
1 small crusty baguette
a few radicchio leaves
black pepper
Hazelnut and Coriander Pesto (see page 32) or a little fruity olive oil

1   Cut the mango either side of the central stone, then remove and discard the skin and the stone. Cut the flesh into slices. Cut the cheese into thin slices.

2   Cut the baguette in half lengthways then arrange the radicchio leaves on one half, letting them hang over the sides. Lay the mango and then the cheese on top. Season with black pepper and drizzle with a little hazelnut and coriander pesto (see page 32) or fruity olive oil. Replace the second half of the baguette to make a sandwich.

3   Cut the sandwich in half to make two sandwiches. Wrap each half in greaseproof paper and cook on HIGH for 1–1½ minutes or until just warmed through. Serve immediately.

TINY CHEESE TRIANGLES

Filo pastry, sometimes spelt phyllo, is a paper-thin pastry made of flour and water. It is possible to make it at home but it is a time-consuming task because of the amount of rolling and stretching needed to make it really thin, so buy it ready prepared and keep it in the freezer until required. When cooked in a browning dish these pastries are lightly browned and crisp. Vary the filling as you like, flavouring the cheese with the suggestions below, or with other ingredients of your choice. Serve as a snack or as a starter before Poached Egg and Coriander Salad (see page 66)

▶ MAKES 12 TRIANGLES ◀

75 g (3 oz) cream, curd or ricotta cheese
15 ml (1 tbsp) lemon or lime juice

▶ *ONE OR MORE OF THE FOLLOWING FLAVOURINGS:* ◀

25 g (1 oz) chopped nuts
30 ml (2 level tbsp) chopped fresh mixed herbs
1 spring onion, trimmed and finely chopped
1 garlic clove, skinned and crushed
25 g (1 oz) chopped dried apricots, dates or figs
a few chopped olives
2.5-cm (1-inch) piece fresh root ginger, peeled and finely grated
salt and pepper

▶ *FOR THE PASTRY* ◀

4 sheets of packet filo pastry, each measuring about 45.5 × 28 cm (18 × 11 inches)
75 g (3 oz) butter or margarine, cut into small pieces

▶ *FOR THE SAUCE (OPTIONAL)* ◀

75 ml (5 tbsp) natural yogurt
15 ml (1 tbsp) tahini
15 ml (1 tbsp) lemon juice
quarter of a cucumber

1   To make the filling, mix the cream cheese and lemon or lime juice with the flavouring of your choice and season to taste with salt and pepper.

2   Put the butter or margarine in a small bowl and cook on HIGH for 2 minutes or until melted.

3   Lay one sheet of pastry on top of a second sheet and cut widthways into six double layer 7.5-cm (3-inch) strips. Repeat with the remaining two strips of pastry.

4   Brush the strips of pastry with the melted butter or margarine. Place a generous teaspoonful of filling at one end of each strip. Fold the pastry diagonally across the filling to form a triangle. Continue folding, keeping the triangle shape, until you reach the end of the strip of pastry. Repeat with the remaining strips of pastry to make a total of 12 triangles.

5   Heat a browning dish on HIGH for 5–8 minutes or according to the manufacturer's instructions.

6   Meanwhile, brush both sides of each triangle with the melted butter or margarine.

7   Using tongs, quickly add 6 triangles to the dish and cook on HIGH for 1–2 minutes until the underside of each triangle is golden brown and the top looks puffy. Turn over and cook on HIGH for 1–2 minutes until the second side is golden brown.

8   Reheat the browning dish on HIGH for 2–3 minutes then repeat with the remaining triangles.

9   While the filo triangles are cooking, make the sauce, if liked. Put the yogurt, tahini and lemon juice in a bowl and mix together. Grate in the cucumber and season to taste with salt and pepper.

10   Serve the filo triangles warm or cold, with the sauce handed round separately.

SPICY CHICKPEAS AND SEEDS

A useful mixture of tasty chickpeas and seeds for nibbling throughout the day or for sprinkling into stir-fried vegetables, pilaffs, stews or salads. I like to serve them along with green and black olives with drinks before a meal.

▶   SERVES 4–6   ◀

45 ml (3 tbsp) vegetable oil
5 ml (1 level tsp) ground coriander
5 ml (1 level tsp) ground cumin
2.5 ml ($\frac{1}{2}$ level tsp) chilli powder
5 ml (1 level tsp) garam masala
2.5 ml ($\frac{1}{2}$ level tsp) turmeric
225 g (8 oz) cooked chickpeas (see page 13) or a 425-g (14-oz) can, drained and rinsed
175 g (6 oz) pumpkin seeds
175 g (6 oz) sunflower seeds
salt (optional)

1   Put the oil and spices in a browning dish and cook on HIGH for 1–1$\frac{1}{2}$ minutes until the oil is hot, stirring occasionally.

2   Add the chickpeas, pumpkin seeds and sunflower seeds and toss to coat in oil. Cook on HIGH for 2–3 minutes until hot, stirring occasionally.

3   Drain on a double sheet of kitchen paper to absorb any excess oil and sprinkle with salt to taste, if liked. Serve cold. Store in an airtight container for up to 1 week.

ONION PAKORAS

There is often confusion between pakoras and bhajias. In northern India, these are served as a teatime snack and known as pakoras, while in the south and west they are known as bhajias and served as part of a vegetarian main meal.

► MAKES 8 ◄

2 large onions, skinned
100 g (4 oz) gram flour
50 g (2 oz) self-raising flour
15 ml (1 tbsp) coriander seeds, crushed
5 ml (1 level tsp) garam masala
5 ml (1 level tsp) ground turmeric
5 ml (1 level tsp) chilli powder
5 ml (1 level tsp) ground cardamom
30 ml (2 tbsp) chopped fresh mint or coriander
salt and pepper
45 ml (3 tbsp) vegetable oil
lemon or lime wedges, to garnish

1   Cut the onions in half, then cut into very thin slices. Put into a large bowl and add the gram flour, flour, spices, mint or coriander and salt and pepper to taste. Mix together.

2   Add about 90 ml (6 tbsp) water and mix together thoroughly to a fairly stiff paste, adding more water if necessary.

3   Heat a large browning dish on HIGH for 5–8 minutes, or according to the manufacturer's instructions.

4   Meanwhile, divide the mixture into 8 portions.

5   Add the oil to the browning dish, then carefully drop each portion of the pakora mixture into the oil using a tablespoon.

6   Cook on HIGH for 2–3 minutes until lightly browned on the underside, then carefully turn over and cook on HIGH for 2 minutes, or until firm and crisp. Serve immediately with lemon or lime wedges.

PÂTÉS, TERRINES & MOUSSES

Until recently the word pâté described a concoction consisting mainly of meat and fat. But now a pâté may be made from fish or vegetables as well as meat. The desire for lighter, lower-fat foods means that vegetable pâtés are becoming popular. They may have a coarse texture or a softer, creamier texture almost similar to a dip. They are no longer served only as a start to a meal but may form an integral part of one large course.

Terrines are rather like firm pâtés, cooked in a loaf dish or terrine then turned out and served sliced. They too have recently gained popularity, particularly the multi-layered, multi-coloured variety.

Vegetable mousses are delightful both to make and to eat. Any purée of lightly cooked vegetables, lightened with egg white and then set with agar-agar, makes a delicious mousse. Turn the mixture into one large or several small dishes, turn out on to flat plates and garnish with salad leaves or herbs before serving.

Breads of all kinds are good served with pâtés, terrines and mousses. Chunky wholemeal, granary or Herb, Cheese, and Olive Bread (see page 117) are good with the coarser pâtés or terrines, while melba toast, pitta bread, oatcakes, rye bread, crackers or toast complement lighter pâté, terrine and mousse mixtures.

GREEN LENTIL AND CREAM CHEESE PÂTÉ

Lentils are the pulse that I most often find myself cooking in the microwave because you do not need to remember to pre-soak them. Here they are cooked until really tender then puréed with cream cheese to make a rugged pâté.

▶ SERVES 4 ◀

100 g (4 oz) green lentils
1 bouquet garni
finely grated rind and juice of half a lemon
large pinch of ground allspice
100 g (4 oz) cream cheese
salt and pepper

1 Put the lentils and bouquet garni in a medium bowl and pour over enough boiling water to cover by about 2.5 cm (1 inch). Cover and cook on HIGH for 20 minutes or until the lentils are really tender.

2 Drain, discard the bouquet garni and rinse with cold water. Purée the lentils in a blender or food processor with the lemon rind and juice, allspice and cream cheese. Season to taste with salt and pepper.

3 Turn into a serving dish, cover and chill before serving.

Pâtés, Terrines & Mousses

Coarse Herb and Mushroom Pâté

Use flat, black, open mushrooms for this pâté as they have the best flavour and give a good dark colour. Mushrooms should never be washed as they absorb water quickly and lose their texture and flavour; likewise they should never be peeled. If they are dirty, wipe them carefully with a damp cloth.

▶ Serves 6–8 ◀

25 g (1 oz) butter or margarine
1 garlic clove, skinned and crushed
2 juniper berries, crushed
700 g (1½ lb) mushrooms, roughly chopped
75 g (3 oz) fresh brown breadcrumbs
60 ml (4 tbsp) chopped fresh mixed herbs such as thyme, sage, parsley, chervil
lemon juice
salt and pepper
fresh herbs, to garnish

1   Put the butter, garlic and juniper berries in a large bowl and cook on HIGH for 1 minute.

2   Add the mushrooms and cook on HIGH for 10–12 minutes or until the mushrooms are really soft and most of the liquid has evaporated.

3   Add the breadcrumbs and herbs and season to taste with lemon juice and salt and pepper. Beat thoroughly together, then turn into a serving dish, cover and chill before serving. Garnish with fresh herbs and serve with granary bread.

Olive Pâté

This makes an unusual pâté with a strong olive taste. Do use good quality olives, preferably the type packed in jars with olive oil rather than those in brine. I like to indulge myself and spread slices of rye bread with cream cheese and then top with Olive Pâté. Yum!

▶ Serves 4 ◀

45 ml (3 tbsp) coarse oatmeal
15 ml (1 tbsp) fruity olive oil
1 medium onion, skinned and finely chopped
1 garlic clove, skinned and crushed
225 g (8 oz) tomatoes, finely chopped
175 g (6 oz) stoned black olives, finely chopped
150 ml (¼ pint) dry red wine
few capers, optional
salt and pepper
olives and capers, to garnish

1   Spread out the oatmeal on a large flat plate and cook on HIGH for 5–7 minutes or until lightly browned, stirring occasionally. Leave to cool.

2   Meanwhile, put the oil, onion, garlic and tomatoes in a medium bowl. Cover and cook on HIGH for 5–7 minutes or until the onion is softened, stirring occasionally.

3   Add the remaining ingredients and cook uncovered on HIGH for 12–14 minutes or until the liquid has evaporated. Leave to cool.

4   Stir the oatmeal into the olive mixture, then adjust the seasoning if necessary. Spoon into a dish, cover and chill before serving garnished with a few olives and capers.

CUMIN AND DAIKON PÂTÉ

Daikon is a white Japanese variety of radish. It looks like a huge carrot with green tops and is milder in flavour than other types of radish. It is used a lot in Japanese cookery, often finely grated and shaped into a pyramid as a garnish and to add flavour. It is available in large supermarkets.

▶   SERVES 4   ◀

900 g (2 lb) daikon or mooli radish
30 ml (2 tbsp) sesame or vegetable oil
15 ml (1 level tsp) cumin seeds
60 ml (4 tbsp) dry sherry
30 ml (2 tbsp) soy sauce
2.5 ml ($\frac{1}{2}$ level tsp) English mustard powder

1   Peel the daikon and chop finely.

2   Put the oil in a large bowl and cook on HIGH for 1 minute or until hot. Crush the cumin seeds and add to the hot oil then cook on HIGH for 1–2 minutes, or until the seeds release their aroma, stirring once.

3   Add the daikon and the remaining ingredients and mix thoroughly together. Cover and cook on HIGH for 20–25 minutes or until really tender, stirring occasionally.

4   Put in a blender or food processor and purée until smooth. Turn into a serving dish and leave to cool. Serve at room temperature.

TRICOLOUR PÂTÉ TRIO

If you want to make a stunning start to a meal, this is the dish to choose. It is a simple idea, consisting of three pâtés each with a distinctive colour—red, white and green. But the secret lies in the presentation, all three are served in the same dish but merge together as one (see the photograph opposite). It is not as difficult as it looks and is achieved by making the pâtés quite soft, spooning each into the dish separately and then shaking gently from side to side so that they merge into one.

▶ SERVES 6 ◀

1 large red pepper
175 g (6 oz) cauliflower florets
300 ml ($\frac{1}{2}$ pint) natural yogurt
300 ml ($\frac{1}{2}$ pint) single cream
1 ripe avocado
15 ml (1 tbsp) lemon juice
salt and pepper
fresh herbs and black olives, to garnish

1 Cut the pepper in half lengthways and remove the seeds. Place, cut side down, on a double sheet of kitchen paper and cook on HIGH for 5–6 minutes or until the pepper is soft.

2 While the pepper is cooking, cut the cauliflower into very small florets and put into a large bowl with 15 ml (1 tbsp) water.

3 When the peppers are cooked, cook the cauliflower on HIGH for 6–7 minutes or until very tender, stirring occasionally.

4 Meanwhile, carefully peel the skin from the peppers and discard. Put the pepper, a third of the yogurt and a third of the cream in a blender or food processor and purée until smooth. Season to taste with salt and pepper.

5 Drain the cauliflower and put into the rinsed-out bowl of the blender or food processor with half of the remaining yogurt and half of the remaining cream, purée until smooth. Season to taste with salt and pepper.

6 Halve the avocado and discard the skin and the stone. Put into the rinsed-out bowl of the blender or food processor with the remaining yogurt, cream and the lemon juice. Purée until smooth. Season to taste with salt and pepper. Leave all pâtés to cool before serving.

7 To serve, put a large spoonful of each pâté side by side into six individual serving bowls. Shake each bowl gently from side to side allowing the pâtés to merge into one another but leaving three distinctive sections of colour. Sprinkle with a few fresh herbs and black olives. Serve immediately with melba toast.

STRIPED VEGETABLE TERRINE WITH SEAWEED

The seaweed used in this terrine is called nori; it is sold compressed into large thin sheets and is available from health food stores. Once sliced this terrine is most attractive and can be served nouvelle cuisine style, as in the picture opposite.

▶ SERVES 4–6 ◀

450 g (1 lb) carrots
450 g (1 lb) parsnips
2 eggs
300 ml ($\frac{1}{2}$ pint) double cream or Greek strained yogurt
salt and pepper
3 sheets of nori each measuring about 20.5 × 20.5 cm (8 × 8 inches)

▶ *FOR THE WATERCRESS VINAIGRETTE* ◀

half a bunch of watercress
150 ml ($\frac{1}{4}$ pint) vegetable oil
30 ml (2 tbsp) white wine vinegar
5 ml (1 tsp) runny honey

1 Roughly chop the carrots and put into a roasting bag with 15 ml (1 tbsp) water. Peel and chop the parsnips and put in a roasting bag with 15 ml (1 tbsp) water. Loosely seal the bags and cook them both at once on HIGH for 12 minutes or until the vegetables are tender.

2 Put the carrots, half the cream or yogurt and one egg in a blender or food processor and purée until smooth. Turn into a bowl and season to taste with salt and pepper.

3 Put the parsnips into the rinsed-out bowl of the blender or food processor with the remaining cream or yogurt and the egg. Purée until smooth and season to taste with salt and pepper.

4 Grease a 1.4-litre (2$\frac{1}{2}$-pint) loaf dish and line the base with greaseproof paper. Spoon in half of the carrot purée and level the surface. Fold one of the sheets of nori in half lengthways and lay on top of the purée.

5 Spoon half of the parsnip purée on top of the nori and level the surface. Fold a second sheet of nori in half lengthways and lay on top. Repeat the layers twice more, ending with a layer of parsnip.

6 Stand on a roasting rack, cover with kitchen paper and cook on MEDIUM for 12–15 minutes or until just firm to the touch. Leave to cool in the dish then turn out on to a serving plate.

7 To make the watercress vinaigrette, trim the watercress, reserve a few sprigs to garnish, and put the remainder into a blender or food processor with the oil vinegar and honey and process until the watercress is finely chopped. Season to taste with salt and pepper.

8 Serve the terrine hot or cold arranged on individual plates in a pool of vinaigrette, garnished with the reserved watercress.

Striped Vegetable Terrine with Seaweed

HERBY AUBERGINE CHEESE TERRINE

Many cookery books insist that aubergines are sliced, salted and drained to extract the bitter juices. Now the quality of aubergines is much improved I find it a waste of time. See the photograph facing page 64.

► SERVES 6 ◄

---

2 large aubergines, each weighing about 450 g (1 lb), finely chopped

450 ml (¾ pint) boiling vegetable stock (see page 15)

2 eggs

100 g (4 oz) breadcrumbs

100 g (4 oz) curd cheese

salt and pepper

60 ml (4 tbsp) chopped fresh mixed herbs

coarsely chopped fresh herbs, to garnish

---

1 Put the aubergine and the stock in a large bowl, cover and cook on HIGH for 20–25 minutes or until the aubergine is very soft.

2 Beat thoroughly to make a purée then stir in the eggs, breadcrumbs, curd cheese and herbs. Season with salt and pepper.

3 Grease a deep 20.5-cm (8-inch) round dish and line the base with greaseproof paper. Spoon the mixture into the dish and level the surface. Cook on MEDIUM for 20–25 minutes or until just firm to the touch.

4 Turn out on to a serving plate and press coarsely chopped herbs on to the sides and top. Serve hot with Sweet Carrot Ribbons with Ginger (see page 99) and baked potatoes or cold with Warm Salad of Green Vegetables with Walnut Oil (see page 68) and warm bread rolls.

CHEESE AND NUT LOAF

The ubiquitous vegetarian loaf! Use a variety of nuts and a strong flavoured cheese for the best flavour. Although the loaf will not be crisp when it is removed from the oven, cooking it uncovered means that it does have something near to a crust. If you prefer it can be crisped and browned under the grill.

► SERVES 6 ◄

---

25 g (1 oz) butter or margarine

1 medium onion, skinned and finely chopped

275 g (10 oz) chopped mixed nuts

225 g (8 oz) hard cheese, such as Cheddar, Double Gloucester, Lancashire, grated

225 g (8 oz) fresh breadcrumbs

10 ml (2 level tsp) finely chopped fresh sage or 2.5 ml (½ level tsp) dried

10 ml (2 level tsp) finely chopped fresh thyme or 2.5 ml (½ level tsp) dried

3 eggs

salt and pepper

PÂTÉS, TERRINES & MOUSSES

1   Put the butter and onion in a medium bowl, cover and cook on HIGH for 5–7 minutes or until the onion is softened, stirring occasionally.

2   Add the remaining ingredients and mix well together. Season to taste with salt and pepper.

3   Grease a 1.7-litre (3-pint) loaf dish and line the base with greaseproof paper. Press the cheese and nut mixture into the prepared dish and level the surface.

4   Stand on a roasting rack and cook on MEDIUM for about 8 minutes or until just firm to the touch. Leave to stand for 5 minutes then turn out on to a plate.

5   Crisp the top of the loaf under a preheated grill, if desired. Serve hot with Tomato Sauce (see page 31) or Cream and Mushroom Sauce (see page 29).

GREEN CABBAGE TERRINE

Blanching large leaves such as cabbage leaves is so easy to do in the microwave, much easier than the conventional method. So here it is used to great effect to bring the leaves to a bright green before they are used to line a terrine. Be sure to rinse with cold water immediately after cooking (in step 1) to preserve the bright green colour.

▶ SERVES 4 ◀

5 large dark green savoy cabbage leaves
450 g (1 lb) curd cheese
about 50 g (2 oz) fresh mixed herbs, trimmed and roughly chopped
1 garlic clove, skinned and crushed (optional)
2 eggs
salt and pepper

1   Put the cabbage leaves and 30 ml (2 tbsp) water in a large bowl. Cover and cook on HIGH for 3 minutes or until the leaves are just pliable and bright green, but not soggy. Drain and rinse with cold water.

2   Grease a 1.1-litre (2-pint) soufflé dish and line the dish with four of the cabbage leaves.

3   Mix the cheese, herbs, garlic and the eggs together, and season to taste with salt and pepper.

4   Pour into the lined dish and cover with the remaining cabbage leaf.

5   Cover and cook on MEDIUM for 8–10 minutes or until the terrine just feels firm in the centre.

6   Unmould the terrine on to a serving plate and serve hot or cold with Pear and Leek Sauce (see page 29) or Tomato Sauce (see page 31).

PÂTÉS, TERRINES & MOUSSES

GRATED CHEESE AND VEGETABLE TERRINE

This is a really simple terrine, simple to make and simple ingredients, but it has a delicious flavour. Grate the vegetables coarsely to give a good texture. Parsnips or celeriac could be substituted for the carrot, but the terrine will not be as colourful.

▶ SERVES 4–6 ◀

15 ml (1 tbsp) vegetable oil
350 g (12 oz) carrots, coarsely grated
350 g (12 oz) courgettes, coarsely grated
225 g (8 oz) leeks, finely sliced
1 garlic clove, skinned and crushed
175 g (6 oz) fresh wholemeal breadcrumbs
100 g (4 oz) Cheddar cheese, grated
3 eggs
45 ml (3 tbsp) natural yogurt
45 ml (3 tbsp) chopped fresh parsley
salt and pepper

1   Grease a 1.7-litre (3-pint) loaf dish and line the base with greaseproof paper.

2   Put the oil, vegetables and the garlic in a large bowl. Cover and cook on HIGH for 4–5 minutes or until the vegetables are softened, stirring occasionally.

3   Add the breadcrumbs, cheese, eggs, yogurt and parsley and season to taste with salt and pepper. Turn the mixture into the prepared dish and level the surface.

4   Stand the dish on a roasting rack and cook on MEDIUM for 25–30 minutes or until firm to the touch. Leave to stand for 5 minutes then turn out on to a serving plate. Serve hot with Roasted Nut and Cream Sauce (see page 30) or Tomato Sauce (see page 31) or cold with salad.

COURGETTE AND AVOCADO MOUSSES

These delicate mousses once turned out consist of a delicious avocado mousse at the bottom topped with vibrant green shreds of courgette. Agar-agar is used to set the mousse. It is the vegetarian equivalent of gelatine and is made from seaweed—don't be put off, it doesn't taste of seaweed! It is available from health food stores. These are best eaten on the day of making because the avocado discolours if kept for longer. Serve as a starter.

▶ SERVES 6 ◀

2 medium courgettes
45 ml (3 tbsp) medium dry white wine
30 ml (2 level tbsp) agar-agar flakes
1 large ripe avocado
150 ml ($\frac{1}{4}$ pint) natural yogurt
salt and pepper
juice of 1 small lime

▶ *FOR THE DRESSING* ◀

45 ml (3 tbsp) olive oil
finely grated rind and juice of 1 lime
lime twists, to garnish

1   Coarsely grate the courgettes and put into a medium bowl with 15 ml (1 tbsp) water. Cover and cook on HIGH for 1–2 minutes or until slightly softened. Drain, and rinse with cold water.

2   Put the wine, agar-agar flakes and 45 ml (3 tbsp) water in a small bowl and leave to soak for 15 minutes. Cook on HIGH for 2 minutes or until boiling, then continue to cook on HIGH for 1 minute or until dissolved, stirring occasionally.

3   Meanwhile, peel the avocados and remove and discard the stones. Mash the flesh with the yogurt and lime or lemon juice. Gradually add the wine mixture. Season to taste with salt and pepper.

4   Grease six ramekin dishes. Divide the grated courgette between the ramekins and pack down with the back of a teaspoon.

5   Pour the avocado mixture on top of the courgette. Cover and chill in the refrigerator for 2–3 hours or until set.

6   To serve, carefully loosen around the edge of each ramekin, then invert on to six plates. To make the dressing, whisk the oil and lime rind and juice together then season to taste with salt and pepper. Spoon a little on to each plate. Serve immediately garnished with lime twists.

CUCUMBER AND DILL MOUSSE

This makes a lightly set mousse held together with a very thick sauce rather than agar-agar, so don't expect it to set completely. It can be served in individual dishes but for more spectacular effect, I like to serve it as a starter in cupped lettuce leaves arranged on a plate and garnished lavishly with cucumber and dill. Hand slices of toast separately.

► SERVES 4 ◄

1 cucumber
225 ml (8 fl oz) milk
1 slice of onion, skinned
1 small carrot, sliced
half a celery stick, chopped
1 bay leaf
3 black peppercorns
50 g (2 oz) white flour
50 g (2 oz) butter or margarine
30 ml (2 tbsp) single cream
30 ml (2 tbsp) chopped fresh dill
2 hard-boiled eggs, shelled and finely chopped
1 egg white

► *TO SERVE* ◄

6–12 cupped lettuce leaves such as radicchio, iceberg, Webb's Wonder
fresh dill sprigs
cucumber slices

1   Finely chop the cucumber and place in a colander. Sprinkle with salt and leave for about 30 minutes. (This helps to extract some of the liquid from the cucumber.)

2   Put the milk, onion, carrot, celery, bay leaf and peppercorns in a medium bowl. Cook on HIGH for 2 minutes or until very hot. Leave to infuse for about 20 minutes.

3   Strain the milk, discarding the vegetables and return to the bowl. Add the flour and butter or margarine and cook on HIGH for 6 minutes or until very thick, whisking frequently.

4   Meanwhile, rinse the cucumber and drain thoroughly. Add to the sauce with the cream, dill and egg. Season to taste with salt and pepper and mix thoroughly together. Leave to cool.

5   When the mixture is cold, whisk the egg white until stiff and fold lightly into the mousse. Cover and chill for 1 hour before serving.

6   To serve, arrange 1–2 lettuce leaves on each plate, depending on their size, and spoon a little of the mousse into each. Garnish with dill and cucumber slices. Serve immediately with thin slices of lightly toasted bread.

TOMATO MOUSSE RING

Substitute the mayonnaise with tofu to add protein or to make a vegan mousse. Fill the centre of the ring with a salad of your choice. I like to make a Greek salad consisting of tomatoes, onions, cucumber, feta cheese and olives and pile it in the middle and then garnish with lots of fresh mint leaves, to make a delicious summer lunch.

▶ SERVES 6 ◀

90 ml (6 level tbsp) agar-agar flakes
60 ml (4 tbsp) white vermouth
700 g (1½ lb) ripe tomatoes, skinned and seeded
2 spring onions, trimmed
300 ml (½ pint) mayonnaise
10 ml (2 tsp) tomato purée
45 ml (3 tbsp) chopped fresh herbs, such as basil, coriander, mint, parsley, chervil
salt and pepper
fresh herbs or salad leaves, to garnish

1 Put the agar-agar flakes, vermouth and 300 ml (½ pint) water in a medium bowl and leave to soak for 15 minutes. Cook on HIGH for 3–4 minutes or until boiling then continue to cook on HIGH for 2 minutes, or until dissolved, stirring occasionally.

2 Finely chop the tomatoes and onion and mix with the agar-agar. Add the mayonnaise, tomato purée and the herbs and mix well together. Season to taste with salt and pepper

3 Spoon the mixture into a 1.1-litre (2-pint) ring mould. Cover and chill in the refrigerator for 2–3 hours or until set.

4 To serve, quickly dip the mould into hot water to loosen the mousse, then turn out on to a flat plate. Fill the centre with a salad of your choice and garnish with fresh herbs or salad leaves.

PASTA, NOODLES & GRAINS

Pasta, noodles and grains all make good bases for many vegetarian dishes. Indeed, all of the cuisines of the world include dishes based on these ingredients, and they are invariably vegetarian. All pastas, noodles and grains make good backgrounds for a range of flavourings having a chameleon-like ability to change from a highly-flavoured Indian or Indonesian creation to something more subtly flavoured, French, Italian or Japanese style. The recipes in this chapter are suitable as starters, main courses, or accompaniments. For sauces suitable to serve with pasta see pages 25–32. Dried foods like these need the same amount of time in the microwave to rehydrate and cook as they do when cooked in the conventional way, but they are easy to cook in the microwave oven. Always use a large bowl and pour over enough boiling water to cover by about 2.5 cm (1 inch). As there is no contact heat (as when cooking in a saucepan) rice and pasta will not stick to the bottom of the pan making it a foolproof method of cooking. On page 13 I've given a comprehensive pasta, noodle and grain cooking chart.
I find that pasta and rice can be reheated very successfully in the microwave. Toss pasta with a sauce, cover and cook on HIGH for 2–3 minutes or until hot, stirring from the outside of the dish towards the centre. When reheating rice add a little water to create some steam, then cook as pasta.

SUMMER PASTA

Requiring minimum effort, this is the perfect dish to make on hot, lazy days in the summer when imported marmande or beefsteak tomatoes are juicy and red, and fresh basil is plentiful. It is not essential to do step 1 in advance but it intensifies the flavours and fills the kitchen with a wonderful basil aroma. Serve as a course on its own with chunks of bread preceded by a selection of dips and crudités (see pages 25–32).

▶ SERVES 4–6 ◀

350 g (12 oz) Brie
3 large ripe marmande tomatoes
1 large handful of fresh basil leaves
2–3 large garlic cloves, skinned and crushed
salt and pepper
450 g (1 lb) spaghetti
45 ml (3 tbsp) olive oil

1   Remove and discard the thick outer rind from the Brie leaving the top and bottom rind on. Cut the cheese into small pieces. Coarsely chop the tomatoes and basil. Carefully mix everything together with the garlic and season generously with black pepper and a little salt. Cover and leave for 30 minutes–1 hour to let the flavours develop.

2 Put the spaghetti in a large bowl and pour over enough boiling water to cover the pasta by about 2.5 cm (1 inch). Cover and cook on HIGH for 7–10 minutes or until tender.

3 Drain the pasta and return to the rinsed out bowl or a serving dish with the oil. Cook on HIGH for 2 minutes or until hot. Pour over the cheese and tomato mixture and toss together. Serve immediately.

MUSHROOMS WITH FRESH PASTA

My favourite way of serving pasta! The combination of dried morel or porcini mushrooms and fresh oyster mushrooms is rich and delicious. Porcini, though expensive, keep their flavour well and are available in Italian delicatessens.

▶ SERVES 4 AS A MAIN COURSE, OR 6 AS A FIRST COURSE ◀

20-g ($\frac{3}{4}$-oz) packet dried porcini or morel mushrooms
225 g (8 oz) oyster, button, cup or flat mushrooms or a mixture, halved
50 g (2 oz) butter or margarine
150 ml ($\frac{1}{4}$ pint) double or soured cream
few green or pink peppercorns, crushed (optional)
1 garlic clove, skinned and crushed (optional)
15 ml (1 tbsp) dry vermouth
salt
450 g (1 lb) fresh pasta
whole lightly cooked mushrooms and fresh herbs, to garnish (optional)

1 Put the dried mushrooms in a small bowl and pour over 150 ml ($\frac{1}{4}$ pint) warm water. Cover and cook on HIGH for 3 minutes. Leave to stand while completing step 2.

2 Put the butter or margarine, vermouth, peppercorns and garlic, if using, in a large bowl and cook on HIGH for 2 minutes.

3 Using a fine sieve, strain the soaked mushroom liquid into the butter mixture. Discard any grit left in the sieve then add the mushrooms to the sauce with the fresh mushrooms. Cover and cook on HIGH for 2 minutes.

4 Put the pasta in a large bowl and pour over enough boiling water to cover by about 2.5 cm (1 inch). Cover and cook on HIGH for 3–4 minutes or until tender.

5 Drain the pasta and mix into the mushroom mixture. Toss lightly together then add the cream and salt and pepper to taste. Cook on HIGH for 1–2 minutes or until hot. Garnish with whole mushrooms and fresh herbs if liked, and serve immediately as a first course, or with a salad as a main course.

STUFFED PASTA SHELLS WITH A TOMATO VINAIGRETTE

The pasta shells I used for this recipe are about 4 cm (1½ inches) long before cooking; once cooked they are much bigger, see the picture between pages 64 and 65. Do not be tempted to use smaller shells—you will need a lot of patience to stuff them and you may find that 20 shells will not be quite enough to serve 4!

► SERVES 4 ◄

20 large pasta shells
900 g (2 lb) fresh spinach, washed, trimmed and chopped, or a 226-g (8-oz) packet frozen chopped spinach
450 g (1 lb) ricotta cheese
freshly grated nutmeg, ground mixed spice or ground mace
salt and pepper

► *FOR THE TOMATO VINAIGRETTE* ◄

150 ml (¼ pint) olive oil
30 ml (2 tbsp) lemon juice
10 ml (2 tsp) tomato purée
fresh herbs, to garnish

1   Put the pasta shells in a large bowl with salt to taste and pour over enough boiling water to cover by about 2.5 cm (1 inch). Cover and cook on HIGH for 18–20 minutes or until tender, stirring once during cooking.

2   Drain the pasta and rinse in cold water. Leave to drain again while making the filling.

3   If using fresh spinach, put it in a large bowl, cover and cook on HIGH for 3–4 minutes or until the spinach is just cooked. If using frozen spinach, cook on HIGH for 8–9 minutes or until thawed. Drain and return to the bowl.

4   Stir in the ricotta cheese and mix thoroughly together. Season to taste with freshly grated nutmeg, ground mixed spice or ground mace and salt and pepper.

5   Use the spinach and cheese mixture to stuff the pasta shells and arrange upright on a serving dish.

6   To make the tomato vinaigrette, whisk the ingredients together and season with salt and pepper to taste. Drizzle over the pasta shells and serve immediately garnished with fresh herbs.

Bundles of Noodles with Oriental Vegetables

Yard-long beans grow until they are very long and thin—hence the name! Well, they're not quite a yard long but can grow up to 30 cm (12 inches) long. They have a delicate flavour and are pliable, enabling them to be bent round and twisted into bracelet shapes (see the photograph between pages 64 and 65). Alternatively they can be cut into short lengths and cooked just like French beans.

▶ SERVES 4 AS A MAIN COURSE ◀

225 g (8 oz) thin wheat noodles
15 ml (1 tbsp) vegetable oil
540-g (19-oz) can sliced lotus root
100 g (4 oz) yard-long beans, or French beans
225 g (8 oz) baby corn on the cob
12 large radishes
small bunch fresh chives or Chinese chives

▶ FOR THE SAUCE ◀

30 ml (2 tbsp) oil
2.5-cm (1-inch) piece fresh root ginger, peeled and grated
60 ml (4 tbsp) plum sauce
15 ml (1 tbsp) mushroom ketchup
30 ml (2 tbsp) dry sherry

1 Break the noodles in half, then divide into 4 bundles. Tie each bundle with the chives. Put into a large bowl with the oil and pour over enough boiling water to cover by about 2.5 cm (1 inch). Cover and cook on HIGH for 12–15 minutes or until almost tender. Leave to stand for 5 minutes.

2 Meanwhile drain the lotus roots and cut the yard-long beans into short lengths and twist into interesting shapes. If using French beans top and tail them. Trim the radishes. Arrange the corn and beans around the edge of a large shallow dish and put the lotus roots and radishes in the centre. Pour over 45 ml (3 tbsp) water and cover.

3 While the noodles are standing, cook the vegetables on HIGH for 5–6 minutes or until tender.

4 Drain the noodles, rinse with boiling water to remove the excess starch and arrange on 4 serving plates. Using a slotted spoon remove the vegetables from the dish and arrange on the plates with the noodles. Quickly add the sauce ingredients and 75 ml (3 fl oz) water to the liquid remaining in the dish and cook on HIGH for 1–2 minutes or until hot.

5 Pour a little of the sauce over the noodles and vegetables and serve the remainder separately. Serve immediately.

PASTA, NOODLES & GRAINS

EGG NOODLES WITH VEGETABLES AND TOFU

Thread egg noodles are sold dried, in cellophane packets in most supermarkets. They are really quick to cook and mixed with any of your favourite vegetables and flavourings such as soy sauce, ginger and chillies they make a good main dish. I have added cubes of tofu and a few nuts to this version to add protein.

► SERVES 4 AS A MAIN COURSE ◄

250-g (8-oz) packet thread egg noodles
60 ml (4 tbsp) vegetable oil
1 medium onion, skinned and chopped
2 garlic cloves, skinned and crushed
2.5-cm (1-inch) piece fresh root ginger, peeled and finely grated
1–2 red chillies, chopped (optional)
2 sticks celery, chopped
2 carrots, sliced
175 g (6 oz) broccoli florets, chopped
100 g (4 oz) beansprouts
a few Chinese leaves or cabbage leaves, shredded
100 g (4 oz) small button mushrooms
100 g (4 oz) firm tofu
soy sauce
black pepper
a few toasted almonds or cashew nuts

1 Put the noodles in a large bowl and pour over enough boiling water to cover the noodles by about 2.5 cm (1 inch). Cover and cook on HIGH for 3 minutes. Drain, and toss with 15 ml (1 tbsp) of the oil.

2 Put the oil, onion, garlic, ginger and chilli, if using, in a large bowl and cook on HIGH for 3–4 minutes or until the onion is slightly softened.

3 Add the remaining vegetables, cover and cook on HIGH for 4 minutes or until slightly softened. Add the noodles, and the tofu, cut into small cubes and cook on HIGH for 2–3 minutes or until hot. Add soy sauce and black pepper to taste.

4 Pile on to a large serving plate, sprinkle with the nuts and serve immediately.

BUCKWHEAT NOODLES WITH EGGS

Sea vegetables have until recently been confined to use in Oriental cooking, but they are now gaining popularity in the West. This dish is based on a Japanese soup and arame seaweed is added to flavour the broth. It is available in health food stores.

► SERVES 2 AS A MAIN COURSE ◄

75 g (3 oz) buckwheat noodles
900 ml (1½ pints) vegetable stock (see page 15)
45 ml (3 tbsp) dry sherry
15 ml (1 level tbsp) dark muscovado sugar
30 ml (2 tbsp) shoyu (unfermented soy sauce)
45 ml (3 tbsp) arame seaweed
1 small carrot, thinly sliced
1 small leek, thinly sliced
2 medium flat mushrooms, thinly sliced
2 eggs

1   Put the noodles in a large bowl and pour over enough boiling water to cover by about 2.5 cm (1 inch). Cover and cook on HIGH for 6–8 minutes or until tender. Leave to stand for 5 minutes.

2   While the noodles are standing, put the stock, sherry, sugar, soy sauce, seaweed, carrots, leeks and mushrooms in a large bowl. Cover and cook on HIGH for 6–8 minutes or until boiling rapidly.

3   Meanwhile, drain the noodles and divide between two large bowls.

4   Pour the hot stock over the noodles, then carefully break an egg into each bowl. Cook one bowl at a time, on HIGH for 1–2 minutes or until the egg is just cooked, then serve immediately.

RISOTTO ALLA MILANESE

A true Italian risotto should have a delicious, creamy consistency while all of the grains of rice are separate and cooked until just al dente. When cooking risotto conventionally the liquid is added slowly and the mixture stirred frequently to prevent sticking. The microwave is perfect for this—dispensing with the need to stir because the lack of contact heat means there is no chance of sticking.

► SERVES 4 AS A MAIN COURSE ◄

75 g (3 oz) butter or margarine
1 small onion, skinned and finely chopped
450 g (1 lb) arborio rice
150 ml (¼ pint) dry white wine
750 ml (1¼ pints) boiling vegetable stock (see page 15)
2.5 ml (½ level tsp) saffron powder or large pinch saffron strands
75 g (3 oz) freshly grated Parmesan cheese
salt and pepper

1   Put half of the butter and the onion in a large bowl. Cover and cook on HIGH for 3–4 minutes or until the onion is softened. Add the rice, wine, stock and saffron, re-cover and cook on HIGH for 13–15 minutes or until the rice is tender and the water absorbed.

2   Stir in the remaining butter and half of the cheese and season generously with pepper and a little salt. Serve immediately, with the remaining Parmesan handed separately, followed by a mixed salad.

RISOTTO WITH ASPARAGUS

Another classic Italian risotto, this time including tender young asparagus. I like to serve it as a main course after a starter of thinly sliced tomatoes, mozzarella cheese and avocado, dressed with a fruity olive oil and sprinkled with fresh basil.

► SERVES 3–4 AS A MAIN COURSE ◄

700 g (1½ lb) thin green asparagus
1 medium onion, skinned and finely chopped
30 ml (2 tbsp) olive oil
350 g (12 oz) arborio rice
about 750 ml (1¼ pints) vegetable stock (see page 15)
90 ml (6 level tbsp) freshly grated Parmesan cheese
50 g (2 oz) butter

1 Cut off the tips of the asparagus about 5 cm (2 inches) down each spear. Peel the remaining asparagus and cut into 5-cm (2-inch) lengths.

2 Put the oil and the onion in a large bowl. Cover and cook on HIGH for 3–4 minutes or until the onion is softened. Add the asparagus stems and the rice and continue to cook on HIGH for 2 minutes.

3 Add the stock and mix carefully together. Re-cover and cook on HIGH for 8–10 minutes or until the rice is almost tender.

4 Lay the asparagus tips on top of the rice, and pour over a little extra stock if necessary. Re-cover and cook on HIGH for 5–6 minutes or until the asparagus is just tender and the rice is cooked.

5 Add the butter and the Parmesan cheese and mix carefully together. Season to taste with salt and pepper. Serve immediately.

BASMATI RICE WITH WHOLE SPICES AND FRESH CORIANDER

Basmati rice should always be served with Indian dishes. It has a distinctive aroma that fills the kitchen. Here pungent spices add to both the smell and the flavour—a word of warning, the spices are not meant to be eaten!

► SERVES 4–6 AS AN ACCOMPANIMENT ◄

30 ml (2 tbsp) vegetable oil
piece of cassia bark
2 star anise
4 black or green cardamom pods, lightly crushed
4 cloves
2 bay leaves
350 g (12 oz) basmati rice
45 ml (3 tbsp) chopped fresh coriander
25 g (1 oz) butter or margarine (optional)
salt and pepper

1   Put the oil in a large bowl and cook on HIGH for 1 minute or until hot. Add the cassia bark, star anise, cardamoms, cloves and bay leaves and cook on HIGH for 2 minutes, stirring once.

2   Add the rice and cook on HIGH for 1 minute then pour over 750 ml (1¼ pints) boiling water. Cover and cook on HIGH for 10–12 minutes or until the rice is tender, stirring once.

3   Stir in the coriander and butter if using, and season to taste with salt and pepper. Serve immediately.

OKRA PILAU

Okra are small green pods, native to Africa, with a delicious flavour. Choose small pods as when they are larger and older they can be tough. When preparing them for cooking cut off the tip of the stem at the end but do not cut into the pod. This preserves the shape of the okra and prevents a slimy substance from being released during cooking. Don't be alarmed by the idea of okra oozing slime— indeed it is a vital characteristic used in the classic American dish called Gumbo!

►   **SERVES 4 AS A MAIN COURSE**   ◄

45 ml (3 tbsp) vegetable oil
1 medium onion, skinned and roughly chopped
2 garlic cloves, skinned and crushed
2.5 ml (½ level tsp) ground turmeric
2.5 ml (½ level tsp) ground cumin
2.5 ml (½ level tsp) ground ajowan or dried thyme
2 bay leaves
1 medium potato, diced
350 g (12 oz) long grain brown rice
about 1 litre (1¾ pints) vegetable stock (see page 15)
225 g (8 oz) small okra
4 ripe tomatoes, chopped
salt and pepper

1   Put the oil, onion, garlic, spices and bay leaves in a large bowl. Cover and cook on HIGH for 5–7 minutes or until the onion is very soft.

2   Add the potato and the rice and mix thoroughly together. Cook on HIGH for 2 minutes, stirring once.

3   Add the vegetable stock, cover and cook on HIGH for 40 minutes or until the rice is almost tender, stirring occasionally.

4   Arrange the okra and the tomatoes on top of the rice and pour over a little extra stock if necessary. Re-cover and cook on HIGH for a further 5–10 minutes or until the rice and okra are tender. Season to taste with salt and pepper and serve immediately with natural yogurt and a pickle or chutney of your choice (see pages 101–104).

GNOCCHI WITH CHEESE

Gnocchi is a favourite Italian dish made from potato, semolina or flour. It is very easy to make and can be made in advance up to step 4. If the gnocchi seem soft after heating in step 5, don't worry, they firm up after grilling.

► SERVES 4 AS A MAIN COURSE ◄

1 medium potato
600 ml (1 pint) milk
175 g (6 oz) fine semolina
100 g (4 oz) ricotta or curd cheese
1 egg
50 g (2 oz) butter or margarine
100 g (4 oz) freshly grated Parmesan cheese
freshly grated nutmeg
salt and pepper

1   Peel the potato and finely grate it into a large bowl. Add the milk and cook on HIGH for 4–5 minutes until hot but not boiling.

2   Gradually stir in the semolina and beat thoroughly together. Cook on HIGH for 5–6 minutes or until very thick, stirring frequently.

3   Add the ricotta or curd cheese, egg, half the butter or margarine and half of the Parmesan cheese. Beat together until well mixed then season generously with nutmeg, pepper and a little salt.

4   Spread the mixture out in a large greased shallow dish (it should be about 0.5–1 cm ($\frac{1}{4}$–$\frac{1}{2}$ inch) thick) and leave to cool.

5   When the gnocchi mixture is cold, cut into 2.5-cm (1-inch) rounds or squares and arrange in a shallow flameproof dish. Cook on HIGH for 2–3 minutes or until heated through.

6   Dot with the remaining butter and sprinkle with the remaining Parmesan cheese. Grill under a preheated grill until golden brown and bubbling. Serve immediately, plain or with a tomato sauce (see page 31).

MIXED GRAINS

Serve this as an accompaniment to make an interesting change from rice or pasta or add grated cheese, vegetables or pickles to make a main meal.

► SERVES 4–6 AS AN ACCOMPANIMENT ◄

50 g (2 oz) butter or margarine
1 medium onion, skinned and finely chopped
100 g (4 oz) pot barley
100 g (4 oz) millet
100 g (4 oz) roasted buckwheat
1.1 litres (2 pints) boiling vegetable stock or water (see page 15)

Herby Aubergine Cheese Terrine, page 50; Sweet Carrot Ribbons with Ginger, page 99
Overleaf: Stuffed Pasta Shells with a Tomato Vinaigrette, page 58

► *TO SERVE—ONE OF THE FOLLOWING FLAVOURINGS* ◄

soy sauce, to taste
grated cheese
grated vegetables, such as carrots, celeriac, courgettes
chopped pickles, such as walnuts, gherkins, capers and a little chopped cucumber and spring onion
salt and pepper

1 Put the butter or margarine and the onion in a large bowl. Cover, and cook on HIGH for 5–7 minutes or until softened, stirring occasionally.

2 Add the barley and half of the stock. Re-cover and cook on HIGH for 20 minutes.

3 Add the millet, buckwheat and the remaining stock, re-cover and cook on HIGH for 20–25 minutes or until the grains are tender and the water is absorbed.

4 Stir in the flavourings of your choice and season to taste with salt and pepper. Leave to stand for 5 minutes to let the flavours mingle, then serve.

WHOLEWHEAT WITH FRESH DATES AND MINT

Wholewheat grains are very nutritious, being high in fibre, protein, iron and B vitamins, and make a pleasant change from rice.

► SERVES 4 AS MAIN COURSE ◄

30 ml (2 tbsp) vegetable oil
2 celery sticks, finely chopped
1 medium onion, skinned and finely chopped
225 g (8 oz) wholewheat grains
large pinch of ground fenugreek
600 ml (1 pint) vegetable stock (see page 15) or water
1 green pepper, seeded and chopped
45 ml (3 tbsp) chopped fresh mint
100 g (4 oz) fresh dates, roughly chopped
45 ml (3 tbsp) thick natural yogurt
salt and pepper
fresh dates and mint sprigs, to garnish

1 Put the oil, celery and onion in a large bowl. Cover and cook on HIGH for 5–7 minutes or until softened, stirring once.

2 Add the wholewheat grains, fenugreek and stock. Re-cover and cook on HIGH for 25–30 minutes or until the wheat is almost tender. Add the green pepper, mint and the dates, re-cover and cook on HIGH for 2 minutes or until tender.

3 Stir in the yogurt and season to taste with salt and pepper. Serve hot or cold garnished with dates and mint sprigs.

65

Overleaf: *Bundles of Noodles with Oriental Vegetables, page 59*
Salad of Oyster Mushrooms, page 67

HOT, WARM & COLD SALADS

Salads need not be cold, sad concoctions of tired lettuce and tomatoes dressed with a harsh oil or salad cream. Today's salads are varied and delicious. They may be cooked beans, grains or pasta tossed in a well-flavoured dressing and served either warm or cold; delicate green vegetables cooked in the microwave oven until just bright green and warm through, but still crisp; or any number of mixtures of nuts, fruits and vegetables.

Warm salads are the new fashion. They are quick and easy to make with the aid of a microwave oven, and provide a delicious starter to serve before a meal that can be prepared in advance (as warm salads must be cooked and served immediately) or they can be followed simply by bread and cheese for a delicious, minimum-effort lunch.

The cuisines of Indonesia, China, Japan and the Mediterranean all include a variety of delicious, well-flavoured salad dishes that we may not normally think of as salad. Gado-gado, an Indonesian speciality, is a mixed vegetable salad with a peanut sauce. To create this, arrange a mixture of raw and cooked vegetables such as cucumber, beansprouts, potatoes, beans and carrots on a large platter and serve with satay sauce (see Vegetarian Satay page 35).

Serve the salads in this section on their own or together as a main dish, a starter or as an accompaniment to a main course.

POACHED EGG AND CORIANDER SALAD

Once you have discovered this method of poaching eggs you will never return to the conventional method. It is essential to prick the yolk to break the surrounding membrane, or it will explode during cooking. Surprisingly, though, the yolk rarely breaks during cooking. Serve this salad as a light lunch dish.

▶ SERVES 2 AS A MAIN COURSE ◀

half a red pepper, seeded
1 small garlic clove, skinned and crushed
45 ml (3 tbsp) vegetable oil
finely grated rind and juice of half a lemon
45 ml (3 tbsp) chopped fresh coriander
selection of salad leaves such as Cos lettuce, Webb's Wonder, endive, spinach, mâche
100 g (4 oz) cherry tomatoes or 4 tomatoes cut into quarters
2 eggs
salt and pepper

1 Cut the pepper into very thin julienne strips and put in a small bowl with the garlic, oil, lemon rind and juice and coriander.

2 Tear the salad leaves into small pieces and arrange on two plates, with the tomatoes.

3 Put 15 ml (1 tbsp) water into each of two small ramekin dishes, and heat on HIGH for 30 seconds or until hot. Break in the eggs and carefully prick each yolk with a cocktail stick or the point of a sharp knife. Cover and cook on MEDIUM for $1\frac{1}{2}$ minutes. Leave to stand for 30 seconds.

4 While the eggs are standing, cook the red repper mixture on HIGH for 1 minute or until hot. Season to taste with salt and pepper.

5 Drain the eggs and place one on each plate. Spoon over the dressing and serve immediately.

SALAD OF OYSTER MUSHROOMS

Oyster mushrooms grow on dead or dying tree trunks. They are much larger than the everyday button mushroom and are oyster-like in shape. They are now more widely available in larger supermarkets and are worth trying as they have a delicious flavour. If you cannot find them, substitute them with flat black or cup mushrooms instead, but do not use button mushrooms as the flavour is not so good. Serve this as a starter or a lunch dish (see the photograph facing page 65).

▶ SERVES 4 AS A MAIN COURSE ◀

25 g (1 oz) butter or margarine
30 ml (2 tbsp) vegetable oil
15 ml (1 tbsp) lemon juice
450 g (1 lb) oyster mushrooms
mixed salad leaves such as frisée, radicchio, mâche
15 ml (1 tbsp) white wine vinegar
salt and pepper
1 small red onion, skinned and finely chopped
45 ml (3 tbsp) chopped fresh mixed herbs

1 Put the butter or margarine, oil and lemon juice in a large shallow dish and cook on HIGH for 1 minute or until the butter melts. Add the mushrooms, cover and cook on HIGH for 2–3 minutes or until the mushrooms are tender.

2 Meanwhile, arrange the salad leaves on four plates.

3 When the mushrooms are cooked, remove them with a slotted spoon and arrange on top of the salad.

4 Quickly add the vinegar to the liquid remaining in the dish and cook on HIGH for 1 minute. Season to taste with salt and pepper. Pour over the mushrooms and sprinkle with the onion and the herbs. Serve immediately.

FAR EAST SALAD

Wood ear mushrooms are a large black fungus that grow on tree trunks. They are used extensively in Chinese cooking and are usually sold dried.

▶ **SERVES 2 AS A MAIN COURSE, 4 AS A FIRST COURSE** ◀

25 g (1 oz) dried wood ear mushrooms
30 ml (2 tbsp) sesame or vegetable oil
1 garlic clove, skinned and crushed
half a head of Chinese leaves, shredded
a few pak choi leaves, shredded
4 spring onions, trimmed and chopped
4 fresh water chestnuts, peeled and sliced, or a 225-g (8-oz) can, drained and sliced
1 Chinese or Comice pear
a few beansprouts
30 ml (2 tbsp) soy sauce

1   Put the wood ears in a large bowl and pour over enough boiling water to cover. Leave to soak for 30 minutes or until swollen and plump.

2   Put the oil and garlic in a large bowl and cook on HIGH for 1 minute or until hot. Add the wood ears and 300 ml ($\frac{1}{2}$ pint) of the soaking liquid, cover and cook on HIGH for 30 minutes until tender. Add the Chinese leaves, pak choi, spring onions, and water chestnuts and cook on HIGH for 2–3 minutes until just softened, stirring occasionally.

3   Meanwhile, core and roughly chop the pear and arrange on 4 plates with the beansprouts. Add the soy sauce to the softened vegetables and mix well together. Spoon on to the plates and toss lightly together. Serve immediately.

WARM SALAD OF GREEN VEGETABLES WITH WALNUT OIL

This is a good example of the new style salads. Lightly cooked green vegetables, more commonly served as an accompaniment, are tossed in a flavoured oil.

▶ **SERVES 2–3 AS A MAIN COURSE, 4 AS AN ACCOMPANIMENT** ◀

350 g (12 oz) broccoli florets
3 medium courgettes
175 g (6 oz) French beans
1 green pepper
▶ *FOR THE DRESSING* ◀
45 ml (3 tbsp) walnut oil
15 ml (1 tbsp) olive oil
15 ml (1 tbsp) lemon juice
30 ml (2 tbsp) chopped fresh mixed herbs
salt and pepper

HOT, WARM & COLD SALADS

1   Trim the broccoli and cut into tiny florets. Cut the courgettes into 0.5-cm ($\frac{1}{4}$-inch) slices. Top and tail the beans and cut into 5-cm (2-inch) pieces. Seed the green pepper and cut into thin slices.

2   Put the vegetables in a bowl with 30 ml (2 tbsp) water. Cover and cook on HIGH for 3–4 minutes until softened but still crisp. Drain and turn into a serving dish.

3   Put the oils and the lemon juice in a small bowl or jug and cook on HIGH for 1 minute or until hot. Whisk together then stir in the herbs and season to taste with salt and pepper.

4   Pour over the vegetables, toss carefully together then serve immediately.

WARM GOAT'S CHEESE, WALNUT AND RADICCHIO SALAD

Use the small round log shaped goat's cheeses for this recipe. They are often sold already cut into thick slices. Be careful to heat them until they are just warmed through or they will melt completely.

▶   SERVES 2 AS A MAIN COURSE   ◀

2 slices Bûche de chevre, each weighing about 100 g (4 oz)
1 small head of radicchio
half a small bunch of watercress, trimmed
30 ml (2 tbsp) walnut oil
50 g (2 oz) walnut halves
30 ml (2 tbsp) lemon juice
5 ml (1 level tsp) Dijon mustard
salt and pepper
chopped fresh chives

1   Heat a browning dish on HIGH for 3 minutes.

2   Meanwhile, tear the radicchio into small pieces and the watercress into small sprigs and arrange around the edge of two plates.

3   Add the oil and the walnuts to the browning dish and cook on HIGH for 1 minute until lightly browned, stirring occasionally. Push the walnuts to one side of the dish, then place the cheeses on the other side. Cook on HIGH for 30 seconds–1 minute or until the cheese is just warm; do not overcook or the cheese will melt.

4   Carefully arrange the cheeses in the centre of the plates and sprinkle the walnuts over the radicchio and watercress.

5   Quickly add the lemon juice, mustard and salt and pepper to taste to the oil remaining in the dish and cook on HIGH for 30 seconds or until hot. Pour over the salad, sprinkle with chives and serve immediately.

SPINACH, MANGETOUT AND CROÛTON SALAD

This is an interesting way to make croûtons and much more pleasant than the conventional deep-fried method. When the croûtons are removed from the oven they will still be soft, but after standing, as if by magic they become crisp.

► SERVES 2 AS A MAIN COURSE ◄

25 g (1 oz) butter or margarine
1 garlic clove, skinned and crushed
salt and pepper
2 thick slices wholemeal bread
75 g (3 oz) small mangetouts, trimmed
75 g (3 oz) small spinach leaves, crushed and trimmed
a few radishes, sliced
50 g (2 oz) Brazil nuts, roughly chopped

► *FOR THE DRESSING* ◄

150 ml ($\frac{1}{4}$ pint) soured cream
15 ml (1 tbsp) lemon juice
50 g (2 oz) blue cheese

1   Put the butter or margarine in a small bowl and cook on HIGH for 10 seconds or until soft enough to beat. Beat in the garlic and season to taste with salt and pepper.

2   Remove the crusts from the bread and spread on both sides with the garlic butter. Cut into 1-cm ($\frac{1}{2}$-inch) cubes, arrange in a circle on a double piece of kitchen paper and set aside.

3   Put the mangetouts in a small bowl with 30 ml (2 tbsp) water. Cover and cook on HIGH for 2 minutes or until slightly softened but still very crisp. Drain and rinse with cold water.

4   Arrange the spinach, mangetouts and radishes on two plates.

5   Cook the croûtons on HIGH for 3–4 minutes or until firm. Leave to stand for 2 minutes or until crisp.

6   Meanwhile, make the dressing. Beat the cream and lemon juice then crumble in the cheese and beat again until smooth. Season with a little pepper.

7   Sprinkle the croûtons over the spinach, mangetouts and radishes and drizzle with the dressing. Sprinkle with the nuts and serve immediately.

ITALIAN MARINATED SALAD

The flavour of this salad improves if left to marinate overnight before serving, but the minimum two hours stated still produces a flavoursome result. Serve as a starter to a pasta main course or as a light meal with a selection of cheeses and some fresh bread.

▶ SERVES 3 AS A MAIN COURSE, 6 AS A FIRST COURSE ◀

6 globe artichokes
30 ml (2 tbsp) lemon juice
150 ml ($\frac{1}{4}$ pint) olive oil
60 ml (4 tbsp) white wine vinegar
1–2 garlic cloves, skinned and chopped (optional)
45 ml (3 tbsp) chopped fresh oregano or parsley
1 large pickled gherkin, chopped
15 ml (1 tbsp) capers
100 g (4 oz) black or green olives, or a mixture of the two
1 small red or yellow pepper, seeded and chopped
1 red onion, skinned and thinly sliced
salt and pepper
450 g (1 lb) cauliflower florets
chopped fresh oregano or parsley, to garnish

1   To prepare the artichokes, cut off the stem and remove all of the tough outside leaves. Cut off all the leaves above the heart then, using a teaspoon, remove and discard the tough spiky choke. Wash the hearts thoroughly in cold water.

2   Cut the artichoke hearts in half and arrange in a single layer in a shallow dish. Pour over the lemon juice and 150 ml ($\frac{1}{4}$ pint) water. Cover and cook on HIGH for 20 minutes or until tender.

3   Meanwhile, mix the oil, vinegar, garlic, oregano or parsley, gherkin, capers, olives, pepper, onion and salt and pepper to taste in a salad bowl.

4   When the artichokes are cooked, drain them thoroughly and mix with the oil and vinegar mixture.

5   Put the cauliflower florets and 45 ml (3 tbsp) water in a medium bowl. Cover and cook on HIGH for 3–5 minutes or until slightly softened but still crisp. Drain and rinse with cold water then mix with the remaining ingredients.

6   Cover and leave to marinate for at least 2 hours before serving, garnished with oregano or parsley.

SALSIFY AND POTATO SALAD

Salsify originally came from central and southern Europe. Black salsify is a newer variety. It is a long thin root with a hard black skin that needs to be peeled before cooking. It has a delicious oyster-like flavour that combines well with potato and a rich mustard dressing to make this one of my favourite salads.

► SERVES 2–3 AS AN ACCOMPANIMENT ◄

450 g (1 lb) black salsify
450 g (1 lb) potatoes
60 ml (4 tbsp) vegetable stock (see page 15) or water

► *FOR THE MUSTARD DRESSING* ◄

60 ml (4 tbsp) mayonnaise
60 ml (4 tbsp) Greek yogurt
15 ml (1 tbsp) wholegrain mustard
30 ml (2 tbsp) chopped fresh parsley or chives
salt and pepper
parsley or chives, to garnish

1 Peel the salsify and cut into 2.5-cm (1-inch) chunks. Peel the potato, if liked, and then cut into 2.5-cm (1-inch) chunks. Put the vegetables in a large bowl with the stock or water, cover and cook on HIGH for 10–12 minutes or until tender, stirring occasionally.

2 To make the dressing, mix all the ingredients together and season to taste with salt and pepper.

3 Drain the vegetables, pour over the dressing, and toss carefully together. Serve warm or cold, garnished with chives or parsley.

LENTIL, RICE AND WATERCRESS SALAD

Cottage cheese and watercress make an unusual dressing for this filling salad. Serve as a side salad, lunch dish or an unusual starter. Add other chopped salad ingredients or lightly cooked vegetables of your choice to make it into a substantial salad main course.

► SERVES 4–6 AS AN ACCOMPANIMENT ◄

100 g (4 oz) green lentils, washed
100 g (4 oz) long-grain brown rice
2 bay leaves
strip of lemon peel
15 ml (1 level tbsp) wholegrain mustard
30 ml (2 tbsp) lemon juice
100 g (4 oz) cottage cheese
$\frac{1}{2}$ a small bunch of watercress, trimmed and finely chopped
salt and pepper
a few sprigs of watercress, to garnish

1   Put the lentils, rice, bay leaves and lemon peel in a medium bowl. Pour over 1.1 litres (2 pints) boiling water, cover, leaving a gap to let steam escape and cook on HIGH for 30–35 minutes or until the lentils and rice are tender. Leave to stand for 5 minutes while making the dressing.

2   To make the dressing, put the mustard into a small bowl and gradually whisk in the lemon juice, cottage cheese and the watercress. Season to taste with salt and pepper.

3   Drain the lentils and rice and rinse with boiling water. Discard the lemon rind and the bay leaf. Turn into a serving bowl, pour over the dressing and toss thoroughly together. Serve while still warm, garnished with watercress or leave to cool and serve cold.

WHEAT AND BEAN SALAD WITH MINT

This is a good example of a recipe that combines two sources of incomplete protein—wholewheat grain and beans—together to make a complete protein. Serve as a main course, as an accompaniment or as part of a meal consisting of a selection of salads.

▶   SERVES 2 AS A MAIN COURSE, 4 AS AN ACCOMPANIMENT   ◀

100 g (4 oz) wholewheat grain
225 g (8 oz) cooked beans such as black-eye, borlotti or flageolet (see page 13) or a 425-g (15-oz) can of beans, drained and rinsed
90 ml (6 tbsp) natural yogurt
30 ml (2 tbsp) olive oil
30 ml (2 tbsp) lemon juice
45 ml (3 tbsp) chopped fresh mint
salt and pepper
225 g (8 oz) tomatoes
half a cucumber
4 spring onions
175 g (6 oz) Cheddar or Double Gloucester cheese, grated
mint sprigs and lettuce leaves, to garnish

1   Put the wholewheat in a large bowl and pour over enough boiling water to cover by 2.5 cm (1 inch). Cover and cook on HIGH for 25–30 minutes or until tender.

2   Meanwhile mix the yogurt, oil and lemon juice together and season to taste with salt and pepper.

3   Drain the wheat, put into a serving bowl and pour over the dressing. Add the beans and toss lightly together. Leave until cool.

4   Roughly chop the tomatoes, cucumber and onions and mix into the salad with the cheese. Serve garnished with a few lettuce leaves and mint sprigs.

HEARTY FEASTS

As the name might suggest, these are all filling main course dishes. They dispel the theory that vegetarian food is dull, boring, monotonous. Here are beans and vegetables combined with spices, flavourings and herbs to make exciting eating.
In a vegetarian diet it is important to eat foods that make complementary proteins. This means that some of these dishes should be served with a bread or grain dish (see Introduction).
For convenience, all recipes containing beans give canned equivalents, although it is preferable in terms of taste and texture and more economical to cook beans from dried yourself (see Introduction). I like cooking beans in large batches as they can be kept for up to a week in the refrigerator or they can be drained and frozen, for inclusion in salads, rice or casserole-type dishes.
Some of the hearty dishes given here are based purely on a selection of vegetables which I have chosen for their flavour, texture and colour. I've often mixed them with eggs, cheese, tofu or nuts to increase the protein value. From the specialised and exotic Yam in Hot Sauce or Green Parcels with Wild Rice and Mushrooms to the more everyday dishes like Stuffed Vegetable Selection and Parsnip and Butter Bean Gratin, there is a meal for every occasion to be found here.

STUFFED VEGETABLE SELECTION

Stuffed vegetables are a popular vegetarian standby as a meal in themselves or served as an accompaniment. There are endless possible combinations of stuffings and vegetables to stuff, the most usual being peppers stuffed with rice. But don't stop there, be adventurous and try stuffing any large vegetables at hand. Try large ripe marmande tomatoes, aubergines, giant Spanish onions, globe artichokes, apples, pumpkins, melons, marrows and courgettes as well as red, green, yellow or black peppers (see the photograph facing page 80).

Each stuffing makes enough to stuff 4 large peppers, onions or tomatoes, or 1 large aubergine, although this varies according to the size of the vegetables used. If the chopped inside of the vegetable is included (see step 1), then the quantity of stuffing will be increased.

Lentil, Cheese and Brazil Nut Stuffing

15 ml (1 tbsp) vegetable oil
1 garlic clove, skinned and crushed
5 ml (1 level tsp) paprika
15 ml (1 level tbsp) tomato purée
225 g (8 oz) red lentils
50 g (2 oz) shelled Brazil nuts, chopped
50 g (2 oz) grated Cheddar cheese

Put the oil, garlic, paprika and tomato purée in a large bowl and cook on HIGH for 1 minute. Add the lentils and 750 ml (1¼ pints) boiling water. Cover and cook on HIGH for about 18–20 minutes or until the lentils are tender, stirring occasionally. Stir in the nuts and cheese and season generously with pepper and a little salt. Use to stuff the vegetables of your choice (see page 76).

Spiced Date, Apricot and Rice Stuffing

15 ml (1 tbsp) vegetable oil
1 garlic clove, skinned and crushed
15 ml (1 level tbsp) garam masala
5 ml (1 level tsp) ground turmeric
175 g (6 oz) long grain rice
50 g (2 oz) dried pitted dates, chopped
50 g (2 oz) no-soak dried apricots, chopped
30 ml (2 tbsp) chopped fresh coriander
salt and pepper

Put the oil, garlic, garam masala and turmeric in a large bowl and cook on HIGH for 1 minute. Add the rice, fruit and 600 ml (1 pint) boiling water. Cover and cook on HIGH for 12–15 minutes if using white rice, or until the rice is tender, stirring occasionally. If using brown rice cook on HIGH for 30–35 minutes, adding an extra 150 ml (¼ pint) water. Add the chopped dates and apricots, re-cover and cook on HIGH for 1–2 minutes until the fruit is slightly softened. Mix in the coriander and season generously with pepper and a little salt. Use to stuff the vegetables of your choice (see page 76).

Wholewheat and Herb Stuffing

175 g (6 oz) wholewheat grain
100 g (4 oz) cream cheese
45 ml (3 tbsp) chopped fresh mixed herbs
salt and pepper

Put the wheat in a large bowl and pour over enough boiling water to cover the wheat by about 2.5 cm (1 inch). Cover and cook on HIGH for 25–30 minutes or until tender. Drain and mix with the cheese and herbs. Season to taste with salt and pepper. Use to stuff the vegetables of your choice (see page 76).

Bulgar Wheat and Tomato Stuffing

225 g (8 oz) bulgar wheat
1 small onion, skinned and chopped
4 large tomatoes, chopped
5 ml (1 level tsp) ground allspice
5 ml (1 level tsp) ground cinnamon
15 ml (1 tbsp) olive oil
15 ml (1 tbsp) lemon juice
salt and pepper

Put the bulgar wheat in a bowl and pour over 300 ml ($\frac{1}{2}$ pint) boiling water. Leave to soak for 10–15 minutes until all of the water is absorbed. Add the remaining ingredients and mix thoroughly together. Use to stuff the vegetables of your choice (see below).

1   Prepare the vegetables for stuffing by cutting a slice off the stalk end to make a lid. Then remove the seeds, core or flesh as appropriate, leaving a shell about 0.5 cm ($\frac{1}{4}$ inch) thick. Halve aubergines and scoop out the flesh. Use the flesh to make soup or stock or chop finely and put in a large bowl with 30 ml (2 tbsp) vegetable oil. Cover and cook on HIGH for 5–20 minutes or until tender (the time will depend on the type of vegetable). Then add to the stuffing mixture.

2   Pile the stuffing of your choice into the prepared vegetables. Arrange in a large dish then carefully pour in a little cold water. If cooking large vegetables such as aubergines or pumpkins you will need to add about 300 ml ($\frac{1}{2}$ pint) water.

3   Cover and cook on HIGH for the times below or cook for 5 minutes then test and cook for a further 5–10 minutes or until the vegetables are tender.

4 large marmande tomatoes	8–10 minutes
4 large peppers	10–15 minutes
4 large onions	15–20 minutes
6 large courgettes	6–8 minutes
1 large aubergine, halved	8–10 minutes
6 globe artichokes	15–20 minutes

4   Remove from the cooking liquid and serve hot or cold with natural yogurt flavoured with a little paprika, garam masala or mint, or with one of the sauces on pages 29–32, and a crisp mixed salad followed by a selection of cheeses.

SPICED MIXED VEGETABLES

This colourful mixture of delicate baby vegetables in a rich spicy sauce is delicious served with wild rice, brown rice and white rice (see the photograph on the cover). For maximum visual effect the artichokes are merely cut in half and served with all of the leaves still attached. This is only successful with small young artichokes—if you cannot find any small ones, then buy four larger ones and cook the hearts only (see recipe on page 71 for preparation instructions).

▶ SERVES 4–6 ◀

▶ FOR THE SAUCE ◀

15 ml (1 tbsp) vegetable oil
5 ml (1 level tsp) ground cardamom
5 ml (1 level tsp) ground anise
10 ml (2 level tsp) ground paprika
2.5 ml (½ level tsp) chilli powder
2 garlic cloves, skinned and crushed
30 ml (2 tbsp) tahini
30 ml (2 tbsp) peanut butter
300 ml (½ pint) vegetable stock (see page 15)
150 ml (¼ pint) thick natural yogurt

▶ FOR THE VEGETABLES ◀

2 baby artichokes
225 g (8 oz) baby sweetcorn
225 g (8 oz) baby turnips, trimmed
225 g (8 oz) baby carrots, trimmed
100 g (4 oz) broad beans
30 ml (2 tbsp) lemon juice
150 ml (¼ pint) vegetable stock
100 g (4 oz) okra
2 small thin aubergines
225 g (8 oz) thin asparagus tips
100 g (4 oz) cherry tomatoes
fresh coriander or flat leaf parsley, to garnish

1   To make the sauce, put the oil, cardamom, ground anise, ground paprika, chilli powder and garlic in a large bowl and cook on HIGH for 2 minutes. Stir in the tahini, peanut butter and stock. Cover and cook on HIGH for 5 minutes or until boiling, then continue to cook on HIGH for 5 minutes. Stir in the yogurt and season to taste with salt and pepper.

2   Trim the artichoke stems and discard. Cut the artichokes in half lengthways. Put in a large bowl with the sweetcorn, turnips, carrots, broad beans and okra and mix together. Pour over the lemon juice and stock. Cover and cook on HIGH for 10 minutes or until the vegetables are slightly softened.

3   Cut the aubergine into 2.5-cm (1-inch) chunks and stir into the vegetables. Re-cover and cook on HIGH for a further 5 minutes.

4   Add the asparagus tips and cook for 2 minutes or until just tender. Then add the tomatoes and cook for 1 minute. Transfer to a serving platter.

5   Cook the sauce on HIGH for 1–2 minutes or until hot. Spoon a little over the vegetables and hand the remainder separately. Garnish with coriander or parsley sprigs and serve immediately with Mixed Grains (see page 64) or a mixture of basmati rice and wild rice.

Green Parcels with Wild Rice and Mushrooms

The choice of casing for these parcels is up to you. Avoid using coarse leaves such as savoy cabbage as they require blanching before cooking. Aim to serve three small parcels per person. The number of leaves required will depend on their size. The parcels are filled with a delicious mixture of wild rice and mushrooms. Although wild rice is expensive, it does have a unique taste and texture.

▶ Serves 4 ◀

1 small onion, skinned and finely chopped

1 garlic clove, skinned and crushed

15 ml (1 tbsp) olive oil

100 g (4 oz) black or cup mushrooms, finely chopped

5 ml (1 level tsp) chopped fresh thyme or a large pinch of dried thyme

100 g (4 oz) wild rice

600 ml (1 pint) vegetable stock (see page 15)

salt and pepper

about 12 large green vegetable leaves, such as Chinese flowering cabbage, Chinese mustard greens, spinach or sorrel

▶ *FOR THE GINGER BUTTER* ◀

75 g (3 oz) butter or margarine

1-cm ($\frac{1}{2}$-inch) piece fresh root ginger, peeled and finely grated

1 small garlic clove, skinned and crushed (optional)

salt and pepper

1 Put the onion, garlic, oil and mushrooms in a medium bowl. Cover and cook on HIGH for 3–4 minutes until the onion is slightly softened, stirring occasionally.

2 Add the thyme and the rice and mix well together. Pour over the stock, cover and cook on HIGH for 35–40 minutes or until the rice is tender. Drain if necessary.

3 Meanwhile, make the ginger butter. Put the butter into a small bowl and cook on HIGH for 10 seconds or until soft enough to beat. Beat in the ginger and the garlic, if using, and season to taste with salt and pepper.

4 Shape into a small pat and chill in the refrigerator until required.

5 When the rice stuffing is cooked, season to taste with salt and pepper. Lay the green leaves on a large flat surface and place two heaped teaspoons of the stuffing on each. Fold the sides of the leaves over the stuffing then roll it up, starting at the narrow end, to enclose it completely.

6 Arrange the parcels, seam side down, in a single layer in a large shallow dish. Pour over 30 ml (2 tbsp) water, then cover and cook on HIGH for 3–5 minutes or until the leaves are just tender.

7 To serve, use a slotted spoon to remove the parcels from the cooking dish and arrange on serving plates. Top each with a portion of the ginger butter and serve immediately.

NUT AND CHÈVRE ROULADE

This method of making a roulade is very successful and produces a stunning result suitable for serving at a dinner party or for a special occasion. If you do not like goat's cheese, substitute it with a soft cheese such as Brie, Camembert or Boursin.

▶ SERVES 6 ◀

▶ *FOR THE FILLING* ◀

225 g (8 oz) small broccoli florets

40 g (1½ oz) butter or margarine

40 g (1½ oz) plain flour

450 ml (¾ pint) milk or half milk and half cream

175 g (6 oz) goat's cheese, such as Bûche de Chèvre

salt and pepper

▶ *FOR THE ROULADE* ◀

3 eggs

175 g (6 oz) Brazil nuts, very finely chopped

30 ml (2 level tbsp) rye flour

1 Line a shallow 23-cm (9-inch) square dish with greaseproof paper.

2 To make the filling, put the broccoli in a large shallow dish with 30 ml (2 tbsp) water. Cover and cook on HIGH for 3–4 minutes.

3 Put the butter or margarine, flour and milk in a medium bowl and cook on HIGH for 5–6 minutes or until thick, whisking frequently.

4 Remove and discard the rind from the cheese. Chop the cheese roughly and stir into the sauce. Season to taste with salt and pepper. Set aside while making the roulade.

5 To make the roulade, put the eggs and salt and pepper to taste in a medium bowl. Whisk until very pale and thick enough to leave a trail on the surface when the whisk is lifted. Lightly fold in half of the nuts and the flour. Pour into the prepared dish and level the surface.

6 Stand on a roasting rack and cook on MEDIUM for 5–6 minutes until just firm to the touch. Leave to stand for 5 minutes.

7 Meanwhile place a large sheet of greaseproof paper on a flat surface and sprinkle with the remaining Brazil nuts.

8 Turn the roulade out on to the paper and roll up loosely with the paper inside.

9 Unroll the roulade and spread with the sauce, reserving about 75 ml (5 tbsp) for the top. Reserve a few pieces of broccoli for the top and sprinkle the remainder over the sauce.

10 Carefully re-roll the roulade and spoon the reserved sauce down the centre. Decorate with the reserved broccoli and a few roughly chopped Brazil nuts. Place on a serving plate and cook on HIGH for 2 minutes or until hot. Serve immediately with a tomato, cucumber and watercress salad.

Red Onion and Gruyère Pie

Red onions have dark purply red skins and the inside layers are edged with red. They are usually imported from Italy and have a mild, sweet flavour, perfect for including raw in salads or for cooking in quantity until soft and caramelised, as here. Serve this delicious pie, which is something between a pizza and a flan, with a salad of mixed leaves dressed with walnut oil and perhaps Salsify and Potato Salad (see page 72).

► Serves 4–6 ◄

30 ml (2 tbsp) olive oil
700 g (1½ lb) red onions, skinned and sliced
10 ml (2 tsp) Worcestershire sauce
175 g (6 oz) Gruyère cheese, grated
salt and pepper

► *FOR THE BASE* ◄

100 g (4 oz) plain wholemeal flour
100 g (4 oz) buckwheat flour
5 ml (1 level tsp) baking powder
30 ml (2 tbsp) chopped fresh parsley
salt and pepper
50 g (2 oz) butter or margarine
1 egg
30 ml (2 tbsp) milk
chopped fresh herbs, to garnish

1   Put the oil, onions and Worcestershire sauce in a medium bowl. Cover and cook on HIGH for 15–20 minutes or until the onions are very soft, stirring occasionally.

2   Meanwhile, make the base. Put the flours, baking powder, parsley and salt and pepper to taste, in a bowl and mix together. Rub in the butter or margarine.

3   Make a well in the centre of the mixture then break in the egg. Add the milk. Gradually mix the liquid into the dry ingredients to make a smooth dough. Knead briefly on a floured surface, then roll out to a 23-cm (9-inch) circle.

4   Place on a double sheet of greaseproof paper and pull up the edges slightly to make a rim. Cook on HIGH for 4–5 minutes or until firm to the touch.

5   Spread the softened onions on top of the base, then sprinkle with the grated cheese. Season generously with black pepper and a little salt, then cook on HIGH for 2–3 minutes or until the cheese is melted and bubbling. Sprinkle with herbs to garnish and serve immediately, cut into wedges, with a selection of salads.

Stuffed Vegetable Selection, page 74

SMOKY STUFFED PAWPAW

Ripe yellow pawpaws are eaten as a dessert like melon. When green and under-ripe, pawpaws make the perfect and surprising receptacle for savoury stuffings. In this filling the slightly sweet flesh makes a refreshing flavour contrast with the smoked cheese (see the photograph opposite).

▶ SERVES 4 ◀

2 green pawpaws
1 yellow pepper
100 g (4 oz) firm tofu
30 ml (2 tbsp) mayonnaise
100 g (4 oz) smoked cheese
salt and pepper
fresh chives, to garnish

1   Prick the pawpaws all over with the point of a sharp knife or a skewer. Cut the pepper in half lengthways and remove and discard the seeds.

2   Put the pepper cut side down on a double sheet of absorbent paper and put in the oven with the pawpaws. Cook on HIGH for 8 minutes or until the pepper is tender. Continue to cook the pawpaws on HIGH for 2–3 minutes or until just tender.

3   While the pawpaws are finishing cooking, put the pepper, half of the tofu and the mayonnaise in a blender or food processor and purée until smooth. Pour into a bowl. Cut the remaining tofu into cubes and mix carefully into the sauce.

4   Cut the pawpaws in half lengthways and remove and discard the seeds. Scoop out the flesh with a teaspoon and roughly chop. Reserve the skins.

5   Add the chopped pawpaw to the pepper sauce and cook on HIGH for 2 minutes or until hot. Cut the cheese into cubes and stir into the sauce. Season to taste with salt and pepper.

6   Arrange the pawpaw shells on a large plate and spoon in the filling. Cook on HIGH for 1 minute or until just hot (do not overcook or the cheese will melt). Cut the chives into 7.5-cm (3-inch) lengths and scatter generously over the pawpaws. Serve immediately with a rice pilaff.

GROUNDNUT STEW

Peanuts or groundnuts are not really nuts but a kind of pulse. In nutritional or protein terms they are second only to soya beans, and contain more protein, pound for pound, than meat or dairy products. Peanuts originally came from South America and are now a major crop in Africa too. Here is an African-style dish including sweet potato and okra in a lightly spiced peanut sauce.

▶ SERVES 4–6 ◀

15 ml (1 tbsp) nut or vegetable oil
225 g (8 oz) shelled peanuts, finely chopped
15 ml (1 level tbsp) mild paprika
5 ml (1 level tsp) ground fenugreek
30 ml (2 tbsp) tomato purée
1 large aubergine
450 g (1 lb) sweet potato
225 g (8 oz) small okra, trimmed
900 ml (1½ pints) vegetable stock (see page 15)

1   Put the oil in a large browning dish and cook on HIGH for 1 minute or until hot. Add the peanuts, paprika and fenugreek and cook on HIGH for 2–3 minutes until the peanuts are browned, stirring occasionally.

2   Put into a blender or food processor with the tomato purée and half of the stock and process until almost smooth. Pour into the browning dish.

3   Cut the aubergine into 2.5-cm (1-inch) chunks. Peel the potato and cut into 2.5-cm (1-inch) chunks.

4   Add the aubergine, potato and okra to the dish with the remaining stock and mix thoroughly together. Cover and cook on HIGH for 20–30 minutes or until tender, stirring occasionally. Season to taste with salt and pepper and serve hot with boiled rice.

WINTER VEGETABLES IN CELERIAC SAUCE

A warming and satisfying stew of hearty winter vegetables. Try to include a good selection from the list below to give a mixture of flavours, textures and colours. Serve as a main course with jacket potatoes and salad, followed by a light dessert such as fresh fruit salad.

▶ SERVES 4–6 ◀

15 ml (1 tbsp) lemon juice
450 g (1 lb) celeriac
1.1 kg (2½ lb) mixture of carrots, turnip, swede, parsnip, kohlrabi, peeled
300 ml (½ pint) vegetable stock (see page 15)
25 g (1 oz) butter or margarine
150 ml (¼ pint) single cream or Greek strained yogurt
salt and pepper
chopped fresh parsley, to garnish

1   Fill a medium bowl with cold water and add the lemon juice. Peel the celeriac and cut into 1-cm (½-inch) cubes, dropping them into the bowl of acidulated water as they are prepared, to prevent discoloration.

2   Drain the celeriac and return to the bowl with 30 ml (2 tbsp) water. Cover and cook on HIGH for 5–6 minutes or until soft.

3   Meanwhile, cut the turnip, parsnip, swede and kohlrabi into pieces measuring about 5 × 2.5 cm (2 × 1 inch) and put into a large bowl with half of the vegetable stock.

4   When the celeriac is cooked, cover the remaining vegetables and cook on HIGH for 15–20 minutes or until tender.

5   While the vegetables are cooking, put the celeriac in a blender or food processor with the cooking liquid, butter and the cream or yogurt and purée until smooth. Add the remaining stock and season to taste. Pour over the vegetables, and cook on HIGH for 2–3 minutes.

TOMATO AND OKRA CURRY

Have an Indian-style banquet and serve this curry with Yam in Hot Sauce (see page 93), Onion Pakoras (see page 44), Hot and Spicy Tomato Chutney (see page 103) and a rice dish of your choice.

▶   SERVES 4   ◀

30 ml (2 tbsp) vegetable oil
2 medium onions, skinned and thinly sliced
2 garlic cloves, skinned and crushed
15 ml (1 level tbsp) poppy seeds
10 ml (2 level tsp) cumin seeds
10 ml (2 level tsp) fennel seeds
5 ml (1 level tsp) ground turmeric
450 g (1 lb) ripe tomatoes, roughly chopped
15 ml (1 tbsp) tomato purée
450 g (1 lb) small okra
30 ml (2 tbsp) lemon juice
10 ml (2 level tsp) garam masala
30 ml (2 tbsp) chopped fresh coriander

1   Put the oil, onion and garlic in a large bowl, cover and cook on HIGH for 10–12 minutes or until the onions are very soft, stirring occasionally.

2   Add the poppy seeds, cumin seeds, fennel seeds and ground turmeric and cook on HIGH for 2 minutes or until the spices release their aroma, stirring once. Add the tomatoes, tomato purée, okra, lemon juice and 150 ml (¼ pint) water. Re-cover and cook on HIGH for 10–12 minutes or until the okra is tender.

3   Stir in the garam masala and the coriander and season to taste with salt and pepper. Serve immediately, garnished with coriander.

CHICKPEAS AND APRICOTS WITH BULGAR WHEAT

The inspiration for this dish comes from the traditional North African dish called couscous, which is a lamb, vegetable and chickpea stew served with millet that has been soaked and is then steamed over the cooking meat and vegetables, usually in a couscousière. However, it is a laborious process and not suited to microwave cooking. This adaptation replaces the couscous with bulgar wheat (a cooked wheat which only requires soaking) and a mixture of chickpeas, vegetables and dried apricots in place of the meat. Serve with extra Harissa Sauce—handed separately for those who like fiery food!

▶ SERVES 4 ◀

350 g (12 oz) bulgar wheat
2 courgettes, sliced
1 red pepper, seeded and chopped
1 green pepper, seeded and chopped
4 large tomatoes, chopped
100 g (4 oz) baby onions, skinned, or 2 medium onions, skinned and quartered
2 garlic cloves, skinned and crushed
300 ml ($\frac{1}{2}$ pint) vegetable stock (see page 15)
30 ml (2 tbsp) Harissa Sauce (see page 32) or tomato purée
5 ml (1 level tsp) ground turmeric
5 ml (1 level tsp) ground coriander
2.5 ml ($\frac{1}{2}$ level tsp) ground cumin
225 g (8 oz) cooked chickpeas or a 425-g (15-oz) can, drained and rinsed
100 g (4 oz) no-soak, dried apricots
25 g (1 oz) blanched almonds
50 g (2 oz) butter or margarine, cut into cubes
salt and pepper

1   Put the bulgar wheat in a large bowl and pour over 600 ml (1 pint) boiling water. Leave to soak while cooking the vegetables.

2   Put the remaining ingredients except the apricots, almonds and butter into a large bowl. Cover and cook on HIGH for 18–20 minutes or until the vegetables are very tender.

3   Add the apricots and almonds and cook on HIGH for 4 minutes.

4   Stir the butter or margarine into the soaked bulgar wheat and cook on HIGH for 2–3 minutes until hot, stirring occasionally until the bulgar is coated with the butter or margarine. Season to taste with salt and pepper.

5   Serve the vegetables and bulgar wheat separately with extra Harissa Sauce (see page 32) if liked.

FLORETS IN CASHEW AND COCONUT CREAM

There are several types of broccoli, the sprouting ones which produce many purple-green shoots and the heading type with one large head like a cauliflower. The purple variety is sometimes sold as Cape broccoli or purple calabrese. Try to include some of each to give a good contrast of colour with the white cauliflower. Once coated in a cashew and coconut cream these delicate florets are transformed into a substantial meal. Serve with Mixed Grains (see page 64) after a first course of Coarse Herb and Mushroom Pâté (see page 46).

▶ SERVES 4 ◀

100 g (4 oz) cashew nuts
450 g (1 lb) cauliflower florets
150 ml ($\frac{1}{4}$ pint) vegetable stock (see page 15)
900 g (2 lb) mixture of green and purple broccoli, cut into florets
50 g (2 oz) creamed coconut
100 g (4 oz) silken tofu
5 ml (1 level tsp) ground cumin
salt and pepper
toasted shredded coconut, to garnish

1   Spread the cashews out on a large flat plate and cook on HIGH for 4 minutes or until lightly browned.

2   Put the cauliflower and the stock in a large bowl. Cover and cook on HIGH for 3 minutes, then add the broccoli florets, re-cover and cook on HIGH for 6–8 minutes or until just tender, but still retaining some crunch.

3   Meanwhile, reserve a few cashew nuts for the garnish and put the remainder in a blender or food processor and process until finely chopped. Add the coconut, tofu, and 300 ml ($\frac{1}{2}$ pint) boiling water and purée until smooth. Add the cumin and season to taste with salt and pepper.

4   Pour the sauce over the cooked vegetables and cook on HIGH for 2 minutes or until the sauce is hot. Sprinkle with the reserved cashew nuts and the toasted coconut and serve immediately with Mixed Grains (see page 64).

Mexican Chilli Beans

Serve these spicy beans as a main dish as suggested below, or spoon into bought taco shells and eat as a snack. The beans can be prepared and cooked in advance, up to the end of stage 3 and then reheated on HIGH for about 4–5 minutes or until bubbling, when required. See photograph facing page 96.

▶ **Serves 3–4** ◀

15 ml (1 tbsp) olive oil
1 onion, skinned and chopped
2 garlic cloves, skinned and crushed
1 green chilli, seeded and chopped
450 g (1 lb) cooked beans such as red kidney, pinto or black beans (see page 13), or two 425-g (15-oz) cans beans, drained and rinsed
30 ml (2 tbsp) tomato purée
450 ml ($\frac{3}{4}$ pint) vegetable stock
salt and pepper

▶ *TO SERVE* ◀

1 ripe avocado
100 g (4 oz) grated cheese
30 ml (2 tbsp) chopped fresh coriander

1   Put the oil, onion, garlic and chilli in a large bowl, cover and cook on HIGH for 4–5 minutes or until slightly softened.

2   Add the beans, tomato purée and the stock, re-cover and cook on HIGH for 7–8 minutes until boiling, stirring occasionally.

3   Using a slotted spoon remove 60 ml (4 tbsp) of the beans and mash with a fork. Return to the bowl and mix thoroughly. Season to taste with salt and pepper, cook for a further 3–4 minutes or until thickened.

4   Meanwhile, peel the avocado and discard the stone. Cut the flesh into neat pieces.

5   To serve, spoon the beans into individual bowls then top each serving with the grated cheese and the avocado. Sprinkle with the coriander. Serve hot with brown rice and Chilli Corn Bread (see page 118) or granary bread.

PARSNIP AND BUTTERBEAN GRATIN

Parsnips, a root vegetable, have a nutty and distinct sweet flavour which permeates anything they are cooked with. This simple but delicious combination of a few ingredients makes a delicious main meal in winter, if served with boiled rice.

► SERVES 4–6 ◄

50 g (2 oz) butter or margarine

50 g (2 oz) wholemeal flour

750 ml (1¼ pints) milk

300 ml (½ pint) vegetable stock (see page 15)

900 g (2 lb) parsnips

4 large carrots

450 g (1 lb) cooked butterbeans (see page 13), or two 440-g (15.5-oz) cans, drained and rinsed

175 g (6 oz) mature Cheddar cheese

salt and pepper

50 g (2 oz) granary or wholemeal breadcrumbs

1   Put the butter or margarine, flour, milk and stock in a large bowl and cook on HIGH for 5–7 minutes or until boiling and thickened, stirring frequently.

2   Meanwhile, peel the parsnips and cut into 2.5-cm (1-inch) chunks. Cut the carrots into 1-cm (½-inch) slices. Add the parsnips and carrots to the sauce. Cover and cook on HIGH for 20–25 minutes until tender, stirring occasionally.

3   Add the butterbeans and 100 g (4 oz) of the cheese and season to taste with salt and pepper. Cook on HIGH for 2 minutes or until the cheese melts. Spoon into a gratin dish.

4   Mix the remaining cheese with the breadcrumbs and sprinkle on top of the stew. Brown under a hot grill. Serve with brown rice or a salad and brown bread.

MUSHROOM, COURGETTE AND BEAN STEW

This makes a colourful and delicious meal. Include button and flat mushrooms for the best flavour and mixed fresh herbs of your choice. When preparing mushrooms, do not be tempted to wash them as they absorb water quickly and lose their flavour and texture—simply wipe with a damp cloth or kitchen paper. Likewise they should never be peeled as most of the flavour is in the skin. See the photograph facing page 113.

▶ SERVES 4 ◀

25 g (1 oz) butter or margarine
1 medium onion, skinned and chopped
25 g (1 oz) wholemeal flour
450 ml (¾ pint) vegetable stock (see page 15)
15 ml (1 level tbsp) mild wholegrain mustard
450 g (1 lb) cooked beans such as flageolet, red kidney, borlotti, or black-eye beans (see page 13), or two 425-g (15-oz) cans beans, drained and rinsed
225 g (8 oz) mushrooms
450 g (1 lb) courgettes
45 ml (3 tbsp) choppped fresh mixed herbs
salt and pepper

1 Put the butter or margarine and the onion in a large bowl. Cover and cook on HIGH for 2–3 minutes or until slightly softened. Stir in the flour and cook on HIGH for 1 minute, then gradually stir in the stock.

2 Cook on HIGH for 4–5 minutes or until boiling and thickened, stirring frequently.

3 Add the mustard, beans and the mushrooms (cut in half if large) and cook on HIGH for 2–3 minutes.

4 Meanwhile, cut the courgettes into 1-cm (½-inch) slices. Stir the courgettes and half of the herbs into the stew. Cover and cook on HIGH for 5–6 minutes or until the courgettes are just cooked. Season to taste with salt and pepper and stir in the remaining herbs. Serve with brown rice or Herb, Cheese and Olive Bread (see page 117).

BEAN MOUSSAKA

Moussaka is probably the best known of the traditional Greek dishes. It usually consists of layers of meat and aubergines, but here is a meatless version containing beans. To complete the Greek theme, serve with a Greek salad, consisting of Feta cheese, tomatoes, cucumber, olives and onions, dressed with a fruity olive oil and oregano. Hummous or tzatziki would be an appropriate start to such a meal and of course a Greek wine such as Retsina.

▶ SERVES 4 ◀

2 aubergines, each weighing about 225 g (8 oz)
15 ml (1 tbsp) vegetable oil
1 medium onion, skinned and finely chopped
1 garlic clove, skinned and crushed
large pinch of ground cinnamon
5 ml (1 level tsp) dried oregano
397 g (14-oz) can tomatoes
15 ml (1 tbsp) tomato purée
salt and pepper
450 g (1 lb) cooked beans such as red kidney, chickpeas, flageolet, haricot beans or a mixture, (see page 13), or two 425-g (15-oz) cans beans, drained and rinsed
300 ml (½ pint) natural yogurt
2 eggs, beaten
grated nutmeg
30 ml (2 level tbsp) grated Parmesan cheese

1 Prick the aubergine all over with a fork and rub with a little of the oil. Place on a piece of kitchen paper and cook on HIGH for 4–5 minutes or until slightly softened. Do not overcook or the aubergine will be difficult to slice. Leave to cool while cooking the filling.

2 To make the filling, put the onion, garlic, oregano, tomatoes and their juice, tomato purée and remaining oil in a medium bowl. Cook on HIGH for 10–12 minutes until the onion is soft and the sauce is slightly reduced.

3 Add the beans and season to taste with salt and pepper. Spoon half of the mixture into a gratin dish.

4 Using a serrated knife, thinly slice the aubergine and arrange half on top of the bean sauce. Repeat the layers once, ending with a layer of aubergines.

5 To make the topping, beat the eggs into the yogurt. Season generously with nutmeg and salt and pepper. Spoon evenly on top of the aubergines.

6 Cook on MEDIUM for 10–12 minutes until the topping is set round the edge but still slightly liquid in the centre. Sprinkle with the Parmesan cheese and brown under a preheated grill if liked. Serve with a Greek salad.

Two Cheese, Spinach and Pinenut Pie

This makes a filling pie suitable for lovers of spinach and cheese. It is not essential to turn the dough out of the dish in step 7, but it does produce a more crusty result. However, if you are feeling unsure of your ability to turn it out in one piece, it can be cooked for the extra 2 minutes, without being removed, and served straight from the dish.

▶ SERVES 6 ◀

▶ *FOR THE FILLING* ◀

1 small onion, skinned and finely chopped
1 garlic clove, skinned and crushed
15 ml (1 tbsp) olive oil
900 g (2 lb) fresh spinach, washed, trimmed and chopped or a 450-g (1-lb) packet frozen spinach
225 g (8 oz) ricotta cheese
1 egg
25 g (1 oz) pinenuts
freshly grated nutmeg
salt and pepper
100 g (4 oz) mozzarella cheese

▶ *FOR THE BASE* ◀

225 g (8 oz) granary flour
75 g (3 oz) strong white flour
2.5 ml ($\frac{1}{2}$ level tsp) bicarbonate of soda
5 ml (1 level tsp) baking powder
salt
300 ml ($\frac{1}{2}$ pint) thin natural yogurt or smetana

1   To make the filling, put the onion, garlic and oil in a large bowl. Cover and cook on HIGH for 3–4 minutes or until the onion is softened.

2   Stir in the spinach. If using fresh, cover and cook on HIGH for 3–4 minutes or until the spinach is just cooked. If using frozen spinach cook on HIGH for 8–9 minutes or until the spinach is thawed. Drain and return to the bowl.

3   Add the ricotta, egg and the pinenuts, mix well together and season generously with nutmeg, pepper and a little salt.

4   To make the base, put the flours, bicarbonate of soda, baking powder and salt to taste in a bowl, and mix well together. Pour in the smetana or yogurt and mix quickly together to form a soft dough.

5   Knead lightly on a floured surface then put into a greased 23-cm (9-inch) flan dish. Using your finger tips push the dough into the shape of the dish, taking it up the sides as well.

6   Stand on a roasting rack and cook on HIGH for 6–8 minutes or until shrinking away from the sides of the dish.

7   Turn out of the dish then stand on the roasting rack and continue to cook on HIGH for 2 minutes or until the base is cooked. Transfer to a large serving plate.

8   Spoon in the filling and level the surface. Cook on HIGH for 3 minutes or until the filling is hot.

9   Meanwhile, coarsely grate the mozzarella cheese. When the pie is cooked sprinkle with the cheese and cook under a hot grill until the cheese is melted and browned.

CHINESE MIXED VEGETABLES

Although this is not a true stir-fry, it is the nearest microwave equivalent. Using a browning dish, even when not preheated, helps the texture of the finished vegetables, but it is not essential. Use a large bowl if you do not own a browning dish.
If you cannot find dried Chinese mushrooms, use button mushrooms instead.

▶   SERVES 4   ◀

50 g (2 oz) dried Chinese mushrooms
30 ml (2 tbsp) vegetable oil
175 g (6 oz) baby corn
1 red pepper, seeded and cut into strips
175 g (6 oz) mangetouts, trimmed
50 g (2 oz) blanched almonds
a few Chinese leaves, roughly chopped
50 g (2 oz) beansprouts
1 garlic clove, skinned and crushed
3 spring onions, trimmed and chopped
45 ml (3 tbsp) Hoi sin sauce
30 ml (2 tbsp) lemon juice
2.5 ml ($\frac{1}{2}$ level tsp) five-spice powder
30 ml (2 tbsp) soy sauce
15 ml (1 tbsp) dry sherry

1   Put the mushrooms in a small bowl with 300 ml (1$\frac{1}{2}$ pints) boiling water and leave to soak for at least 30 minutes.

2   Put the oil in a browning dish or a large bowl with the corn and cook on HIGH for 2–3 minutes or until slightly softened.

3   Add the mangetouts, almonds, Chinese leaves, beansprouts, garlic, spring onions, Hoi sin sauce, lemon juice, five-spice powder, soy sauce and sherry and mix thoroughly together.

4   Stir in the drained mushrooms. Cover and cook on HIGH for 3 minutes or until the vegetables are softened, stirring occasionally. Serve immediately with noodles or rice.

POTATO, CHEESE AND LEEK BAKE

The combination of cheese and leeks is always popular. When selecting leeks, choose the smaller ones, which are most tender. They should look white at the root end, with crisp, green tops. Wash thoroughly in several changes of water as they hold a surprising amount of dirt between their layers.

▶ SERVES 2 ◀

900 g (2 lb) potatoes
700 g (1½ lb) leeks
450 ml (¾ pint) vegetable stock (see page 15)
225 g (8 oz) Gruyère cheese
45 ml (3 tbsp) chopped fresh parsley
salt and pepper
45 ml (3 tbsp) brown breadcrumbs
45 ml (3 tbsp) freshly grated Parmesan cheese

1   Peel the potatoes, if liked, and cut into 1-cm (½-inch) cubes. Trim the leeks and cut into 1-cm (½-inch) slices.

2   Put the potatoes, leeks and stock in a large bowl. Cover and cook on HIGH for 20–25 minutes or until tender, stirring occasionally.

3   Meanwhile, cut the cheese into 1-cm (½-inch) cubes. Mix the cheese into the leek and potato mixture with the parsley. Season to taste with salt and pepper. Turn into 2 individual gratin dishes and level the surfaces.

4   Cook on HIGH for 1–2 minutes or until hot (do not overcook or the cheese will melt). Sprinkle with the breadcrumbs and Parmesan, then brown under a hot grill. Serve with a crunchy mixed salad.

RATATOUILLE

Ratatouille is a classic Provençal casserole of courgettes, peppers, onions, aubergines and tomatoes. It is a versatile dish and can be served hot on its own as a main dish or cold, or as an accompaniment.
Serve four as a main course.

▶ SERVES 4 ◀

75 ml (3 tbsp) olive oil
450 g (1 lb) onions, skinned and thinly sliced
1 garlic clove, skinned and crushed
450 g (1 lb) tomatoes, skinned, seeded and chopped, or one 397-g (14-oz) can tomatoes with their juice
2 red or green peppers, seeded and sliced
450 g (1 lb) courgettes, sliced
450 g (1 lb) aubergines, thinly sliced
30 ml (2 tbsp) tomato purée
salt and pepper
bouquet garni

1   Put the oil in a large bowl with the onions and the garlic. Cover and cook on HIGH for 5–7 minutes until soft.

2   Add the remaining ingredients, cover and cook on HIGH for 25–30 minutes. The vegetables should be soft and well mixed but retain their shape and most of the cooking liquid should have evaporated. Serve hot or cold.

YAM IN HOT SAUCE

Yams look like large, hairy, irregularly shaped potatoes with a coarse dark brown, terracotta or pink tinged skin and creamy white flesh. They originated in Africa but have now become widely available in British markets and supermarkets. They taste similar to potatoes and combine well with hot, spicy flavours as here.

▶   SERVES 4   ◀

15 ml (1 tbsp) vegetable oil
2 garlic cloves, skinned and crushed
10 ml (2 level tsp) ground turmeric
10 ml (2 level tsp) ground cumin
10 ml (2 level tsp) ground coriander
2 black cardamoms
a few curry leaves (optional)
1 green chilli, seeded and chopped
450 g (1 lb) ripe tomatoes, roughly chopped
2 onions, skinned and thinly sliced
700 g (1½ lb) yam
1 green pepper, seeded and sliced
300 ml (½ pint) vegetable stock (see page 15)
salt and pepper

1   Put the oil, garlic, spices, curry leaves and chilli in a large bowl and cook on HIGH for 2 minutes until sizzling, stirring occasionally.

2   Add the tomatoes and the onion, cover and cook on HIGH for 5–7 minutes until the tomatoes and onions are very soft, stirring occasionally. Set aside while cooking the yam.

3   Prick the yam all over using the point of a sharp knife or a skewer. Wrap loosely in kitchen paper and cook on HIGH for 20 minutes or until the yam feels soft when gently squeezed.

4   Using a sharp knife and holding the yam in a teatowel, carefully remove the skin from the yam and discard. Cut the flesh into neat cubes and stir into the sauce with the green pepper and the stock.

5   Cover and cook on HIGH for 5–6 minutes or until very hot. Season to taste with salt and pepper. Serve with Basmati Rice with Whole Spices and Fresh Coriander (see page 62) or any rice dish with Whole Baked Plantains (see page 98).

HEARTY FEASTS

LAYERED SEAWEED CAKE

*Nori is a kind of seaweed widely available in health food stores as large sheets.
For this recipe you will need large round sheets—if you cannot buy these already
prepared, then simply buy the squares and cut into circles yourself.*

▶ SERVES 6–8 ◀

350 g (12 oz) short grain white or brown rice
15 ml (1 tbsp) shoyu (naturally fermented soy sauce)
30 ml (2 tbsp) white wine vinegar
30 ml (2 tbsp) runny honey
15 ml (1 tbsp) mirin or dry sherry
1 ripe avocado, peeled and finely chopped
1 small red pepper, seeded and finely chopped
half a cucumber, chopped
seven 18-cm (7-inch) round sheets of nori

▶ *FOR THE SAUCE* ◀

90 ml (6 tbsp) shoyu (naturally fermented soy sauce)
30 ml (2 tbsp) mirin or dry sherry
1 garlic clove, skinned and crushed
1 spring onion, trimmed and finely chopped
10 ml (2 tsp) runny honey
1 small mooli, 2 large carrots, to serve (optional)

1 Put the rice and salt to taste in a large bowl. Pour over enough boiling water to cover by about 2.5 cm (1 inch), cover and cook on HIGH for 15 minutes if using white rice, or 30–35 minutes if using brown rice.

2 Tip the rice into a colander or sieve and leave to drain.

3 Meanwhile put the shoyu, vinegar, honey and mirin into the bowl and cook on HIGH for 1–2 minutes or until the honey has melted. Return the rice to the bowl and stir lightly with a fork to coat in the sauce. Leave to cool.

4 Meanwhile, make the sauce. Mix the shoyu, mirin, garlic, spring onion and honey together.

5 When the rice is cool, divide into three. Mix the avocado into one third, the pepper into a second third and the cucumber into the last third.

6 Cut the nori into 18-cm (7-inch) circles if necessary (see introduction) and place two on a large flat serving plate. Spread with one of the rice mixtures. Top with two more sheets of nori and spread with a second rice mixture. Repeat with two more sheets of nori and the remaining rice mixture. Top with the remaining sheet of nori. Serve the rice cake in wedges, with the sauce and the mooli and carrot, cut into shapes, handed separately.

WALNUT AND MATZO BALLS WITH TARRAGON SAUCE

Matzo meal is made from ground matzos or unleavened crispbreads. It is popular at the time of Jewish passover when it is used in place of leavened breadcrumbs. It has a pleasant, distinctive flavour and can be bought in bags in supermarkets that stock kosher foodstuffs. Serve with Spiced Red Cabbage with Tangerines (see page 98).

► **SERVES 4** ◄

225 g (8 oz) walnut halves
1 medium onion, skinned and roughly chopped
25 g (1 oz) rolled oats
50 g (2 oz) matzo meal
100 g (4 oz) curd cheese
15 ml (1 tbsp) mild wholegrain mustard
1 egg
salt and pepper

► *FOR THE TARRAGON SAUCE* ◄

60 ml (4 tbsp) medium dry white wine
300 ml ($\frac{1}{2}$ pint) double cream
45 ml (3 tbsp) chopped fresh tarragon
salt and pepper
fresh tarragon, to garnish

1 Put the walnuts and onion in a blender or food processor and process until very finely chopped. Add the oats, matzo meal, curd cheese, mustard and the egg and continue to process until well mixed. Season to taste with salt and pepper.

2 Shape the mixture into 16 walnut-sized balls and arrange around the edge of a large flat plate.

3 To make the sauce, put the wine in a medium bowl and cook on HIGH for 3–4 minutes or until reduced by half. Stir in the cream and tarragon.

4 Cook the walnut and matzo balls on HIGH for 8–9 minutes or until firm to the touch.

5 Cook the sauce on HIGH for 1–2 minutes or until hot. Serve immediately with the walnut and matzo balls, garnished with tarragon.

VEGETABLE ACCOMPANIMENTS

The new style of informal eating, vegetarian or otherwise, relies less on a rigid three-course structure and a pudding, and focuses more on presenting several dishes to be eaten together as one course. Many of the recipes in this chapter are good as side dishes to add colour, interest or flavour but some work equally well as a light meal or a course on their own.

Vegetables cooked in the microwave are full of colour, flavour and texture and far superior to the overboiled tasteless items more usually served. Follow the charts on page 10 to cook vegetables to perfection and then serve au naturel or with one of the sauces on pages 29–31. Alternatively you can serve them as I do with a generous knob of butter (or margarine) flavoured with chopped fresh herbs, ginger, garlic or your favourite spice, or sprinkle them with toasted nuts or coconut or spiced chickpeas and seeds (see page 43). Another alternative is to sprinkle them generously with a grated hard cheese such as Cheddar or Parmesan.

GLAZED SWEET AND SOUR COURGETTES

If you are feeling creative, score the skin of the courgettes with a cannelle knife to make an attractive pattern. Serve with Bean and Rice Burgers (see page 38) or baked potatoes filled with cheese.

► SERVES 4 ◄

150 ml ($\frac{1}{4}$ pint) unsweetened pineapple juice
15 ml (1 level tbsp) dark muscovado sugar
15 ml (1 tbsp) soy sauce
30 ml (2 tbsp) cider vinegar
450 g (1 lb) baby courgettes
5 ml (1 level tsp) potato flour

1 Put the pineapple juice, sugar, soy sauce and vinegar in a medium bowl and cook on HIGH for 4 minutes or until slightly reduced.

2 If the courgettes are large, cut them in half. Add to the sauce, cover and cook on HIGH for 3–4 minutes or until the courgettes are just tender.

3 Sprinkle with the potato flour and cook for 1 minute until the sauce has thickened slightly, stirring occasionally. Serve immediately.

Mexican Chilli Beans, page 86; Chilli Corn Bread, page 118

Button Mushrooms with Red Wine and Crushed Coriander

Coriander seeds are the roasted fruit of an annual plant grown in southern Europe and the Middle East. They have a mild, sweet orangey flavour and a pungent aroma. As with all whole spices, they should be crushed just before cooking to release the flavour and aroma.

▶ Serves 4–6 ◀

30 ml (2 level tbsp) coriander seeds
2 large garlic cloves, skinned and crushed
150 ml ($\frac{1}{4}$ pint) dry red wine
700 g ($1\frac{1}{2}$ lb) button mushrooms
salt and pepper
chopped fresh coriander, to garnish

1 Crush the coriander seeds using a pestle and mortar, then put in a large bowl with the garlic and red wine. Cook on HIGH for 3 minutes or until the wine is bubbling.

2 Add the whole mushrooms, cover and cook on HIGH for 8–10 minutes or until the mushrooms are tender, stirring occasionally. Season to taste with salt and pepper. Sprinkle generously with chopped fresh coriander. Serve hot or cold, as an accompaniment, or eat with bread to mop up the juices as a snack or light meal.

Grated Celeriac Sauté with Apples and Hazelnuts

Celeriac is a variety of celery, grown for its thick tuberous root. It has pleasant white flesh and a mild celery-like flavour. Here it is coarsely grated and cooked briefly until just hot, to make a delicious accompaniment to most main dishes.

▶ Serves 4–6 ◀

60 ml (4 tbsp) nut or vegetable oil
50 g (2 oz) hazelnuts, roughly chopped
450 g (1 lb) celeriac, peeled and coarsely grated
2 large red eating apples, cored and roughly chopped
squeeze of lemon juice
salt and pepper

1 Put the oil in a large shallow dish or browning dish and cook on HIGH for 1 minute or until hot. Add the nuts and cook on HIGH for 3–4 minutes, or until lightly browned, stirring occasionally.

2 Add the celeriac, apples and a little lemon juice and cook on HIGH for 3–4 minutes or until just hot and slightly softened, stirring occasionally. Season with salt and pepper and serve immediately.

Fruit and Polenta Pudding, page 111

VEGETABLE ACCOMPANIMENTS

SPICED RED CABBAGE WITH TANGERINES

This makes a striking contrast of flavours and colours and a pleasant change from green cabbage. If you have firm tangerines or satsumas, slice the fruit, instead of segmenting it to expose more of the bright orange colour.

► SERVES 6 ◄

5 tangerines or satsumas
1 medium onion, skinned
150 ml ($\frac{1}{4}$ pint) dry red wine
30 ml (2 level tsp) light muscovado sugar
2.5–5 ml ($\frac{1}{2}$–1 level tsp) ground mixed spice
900 g (2 lb) red cabbage
salt and pepper

1   Finely grate the rind and squeeze the juice from two of the tangerines into a large bowl. Peel and segment the remaining tangerines and set aside.

2   Cut the onion in half and then into thin slices. Mix with the tangerine rind and juice. Add the wine, sugar and spice and mix well together. Cover and cook on HIGH for 4–5 minutes or until the onion is slightly softened.

3   Meanwhile remove the tough central core from the cabbage and discard. Cut the cabbage into 2.5-cm (1-inch) chunks and separate the layers.

4   Add to the softened onion, re-cover and cook on HIGH for 13 minutes or until the cabbage is tender, stirring occasionally. Add the tangerine segments and cook on HIGH for 2 minutes or until just hot. Season to taste with salt and pepper and serve immediately.

WHOLE BAKED PLANTAINS

The plantain is a member of the banana family and a staple food in tropical regions. It is the same basic shape as a banana, but usually larger and heavier with three or four clearly defined sides rather than four or five sides like a banana. Unlike the banana, it is always eaten cooked, as a vegetable. Cooked whole, in their skins, they become deliciously soft and succulent with a slightly sweet banana-potato flavour. Serve with any spicy dishes.

► SERVES 2–4 ◄

2 large plantains with speckled brown-black skins
Harissa sauce, or chutney, to serve (optional, see introduction)

1   Prick the plantains all over with a fork or the point of a sharp knife. Cook on HIGH for 7–8 minutes or until the plantains feel soft when squeezed gently and a little liquid begins to ooze out of the pricked holes.

2   To serve, split the skin lengthways and eat straight from the skin with a little Harissa Sauce (see page 32) or chutney, or serve with spicy dishes.

PIPERANA

This colourful mixture of softened peppers is served cold and goes well with a selection of salad dishes and French bread.

► SERVES 4 ◄

2 red peppers
2 yellow peppers
2 green peppers
2 large garlic cloves, skinned and crushed
1 shallot, skinned and finely chopped
75 ml (5 tbsp) olive oil
30 ml (2 tbsp) lemon juice
45 ml (3 tbsp) chopped fresh mixed herbs such as marjoram, thyme, parsley
pinch of sugar
salt and pepper

1   Cut the peppers in half lengthways and remove and discard the seeds and the cores. Arrange six halves in a circle, cut-side down on a double sheet of kitchen paper and cook on HIGH for 10–12 minutes or until really soft. Repeat with the remaining peppers.

2   Remove the skins, if wished, then cut the peppers into thin strips.

3   Mix the garlic, onion, oil, lemon juice, herbs and sugar together with salt and pepper to taste. Arrange the peppers on a plate. Pour over the dressing, then leave to stand for at least 10 minutes before serving.

SWEET CARROT RIBBONS WITH GINGER

Use a U-shaped potato peeler with a swivel blade to achieve wafer thin ribbons of carrot. Although this takes a little longer than slicing, the cooking time is greatly reduced and the finished effect is worthwhile. They make a delicious accompaniment to Herby Aubergine Terrine (see page 50 and see the picture facing page 64).

► SERVES 4–6 ◄

700 g (1½ lb) large carrots, scraped
30 ml (2 tbsp) runny honey
2.5 ml (½ level tsp) Dijon mustard
25 g (1 oz) butter or margarine
1-cm (½-inch) piece fresh root ginger, peeled and grated

1   Using a potato peeler, slice the carrots lengthways into wafer thin strips.

2   Put the honey, mustard, butter or margarine and ginger in a large bowl and cook on HIGH for 3 minutes, stirring once. Add the carrots and cook on HIGH for 1–2 minutes, until just hot, stirring once. Serve immediately.

MIXED VEGETABLE PLATTER WITH HOLLANDAISE

It is essential to follow these instructions for making Hollandaise exactly, even to the point of using the correct size bowl (see page 14). Make sure that you have all of the ingredients ready for making the sauce before the vegetables are cooked so that the sauce and vegetables can be served together while still both hot. Use other small vegetables of your choice, if preferred, and serve with a simple main dish such as a cold terrine, or serve as a starter

▶ SERVES 4 ◀

225 g (8 oz) broccoli florets, trimmed

225 g (8 oz) carrots, scrubbed

2 medium courgettes, trimmed

50 g (2 oz) mangetouts, topped and tailed

½ red pepper, sliced

▶ *FOR THE HOLLANDAISE SAUCE* ◀

100 g (4 oz) butter, cut into small pieces

2 egg yolks

30 ml (2 tbsp) white wine vinegar

white pepper

1 Arrange the broccoli florets around the edge of a large shallow dish, with the stems facing towards the outside.

2 Cut the carrots into 5-cm (2-inch) long strips, and place in the middle of the dish. Sprinkle with 45 ml (3 tbsp) of water. Cover and cook on HIGH for 2–3 minutes or until the vegetables are only just tender.

3 Meanwhile, cut the courgettes into 0.5-cm (¼-inch) slices. Put the courgettes, mangetouts and pepper in the middle of the dish with the carrots. Re-cover and cook on HIGH for 2 minutes or until all of the vegetables are just tender. Leave covered while making the Hollandaise sauce.

4 Meanwhile prepare the ingredients for the Hollandaise.

5 When the vegetables are cooked, leave to stand covered, while finishing the Hollandaise.

6 To make the Hollandaise, put the butter into a large bowl (see page 14) and cook on HIGH for 30 seconds–1 minute until just melted (do not cook for any longer or the butter will be too hot and the mixture will curdle).

7 Add the egg yolks and the vinegar and whisk together until well mixed. Cook on HIGH for 1–1½ minutes, whisking every 15 seconds until thick enough to coat the back of a spoon. Season with a little pepper and serve immediately with the vegetables.

QUICK PICKLES, CHUTNEYS & RELISHES

The microwave oven is ideal for making all kinds of preserves as smaller quantities can be made to order. Because there is no direct heat the food does not get stuck to the bowl, as in traditional preserve making. As with all foods high in sugar, it is essential to use a heatproof bowl and to wear oven gloves when removing the bowl from the oven.

To convert your favourite recipe, reduce the quantity to a suitable amount, then use the conventional recipe as a guide to the method of preparation. Cook in a large bowl on HIGH until sufficiently cooked or setting point is reached.

The preserves in this chapter are designed to be made and eaten almost immediately. Cooking times are kept to a minimum and they do not require maturing time before being eaten. As the quantities made are quite small they can be stored, covered, in the refrigerator and used (within two weeks) when required. However, if you do wish to keep them for longer, pack into sterile jars and seal properly. Jars can be prepared for potting in the microwave. To do this, fill very clean jars a quarter full with water and cook on HIGH until boiling rapidly. Remove from the oven, pour out the water then leave to dry upturned on a clean teatowel. Pour the preserve into the warm, sterile jars then cover with a wax paper disc and a cellophane cover.

THREE PEPPER RELISH

A very hot relish to pep up bland foods. Hoi sin sauce is a spicy sauce much used in Chinese cookery; find it on the Chinese counter in larger supermarkets.

▶ MAKES ABOUT 350 g (12 oz) ◀

1 medium onion, skinned and chopped
2 red peppers, seeded and chopped
1 red chilli, chopped
30 ml (2 tbsp) vegetable oil
2 garlic cloves, skinned and thinly sliced
15 ml (1 level tbsp) light muscovado sugar
30 ml (2 tbsp) lime juice
15 ml (1 tbsp) Hoi sin sauce
15 ml (1 level tbsp) ground paprika
salt

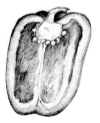

1 Put all the ingredients in a large bowl and mix thoroughly together.

2 Cook on HIGH for 10–15 minutes or until the vegetables are soft, stirring occasionally. Cool, then transfer to a jar or bowl, cover and store in the refrigerator for up to 2 weeks.

QUICK PICKLES, CHUTNEYS & RELISHES

CARROT AND RAISIN CHUTNEY

An unusual sweet and sour chutney, good served with vegetable terrines. Or stir a few tablespoonfuls into thick Greek yogurt to make an interesting raita to serve with curries or as a sauce with vegetable pâtés or stuffed vegetables, or as a dressing for a mixed salad of your own invention.

▶ MAKES ABOUT 450 g (1 lb) ◀

450 g (1 lb) carrots, coarsely grated
100 g (4 oz) raisins
15 ml (1 level tbsp) black poppy seeds
2 bay leaves
2.5 ml ($\frac{1}{2}$ level tsp) ground mixed spice
2.5 ml ($\frac{1}{2}$ level tsp) ground ginger
4 black peppercorns
50 g (2 oz) dark muscovado sugar
300 ml ($\frac{1}{2}$ pint) white wine vinegar

1 Put all the ingredients in a large bowl and cook on HIGH for 12–15 minutes until the carrots are tender and the liquid has evaporated.

2 Leave to cool, then pack into a clean jar, cover and store in the refrigerator for up to 2 weeks. Or pack in sterile jars and seal (see introduction).

INDONESIAN VEGETABLE PICKLE

An attractive mixture of crunchy vegetables, sesame seeds and nuts. Serve with Vegetarian Satay (see page 35) or noodle dishes. Spiced pickling vinegar is available in most supermarkets or you can make your own by bringing 600 ml (1 pint) malt, wine or distilled vinegar to the boil with 50 g (2 oz) pickling spice. Leave to marinate for at least 2 hours or overnight then strain through muslin into bottles and seal with vinegar-proof tops.

▶ MAKES ABOUT 750 g (1$\frac{1}{2}$ lb) ◀

1-cm ($\frac{1}{2}$-inch) piece fresh root ginger, peeled and grated
2 large garlic cloves, skinned and crushed
10 ml (2 level tsp) ground turmeric
45 ml (3 tbsp) vegetable oil
150 ml ($\frac{1}{4}$ pint) spiced pickling vinegar
1–2 green chillies, seeded and sliced
half a cucumber
60 ml (4 level tbsp) sesame seeds
2 large carrots
175 g (6 oz) cauliflower florets
100 g (4 oz) dark muscovado sugar
60 ml (4 tbsp) sesame seeds
100 g (4 oz) salted peanuts, roughly chopped

1 Put the ginger, garlic, turmeric and oil in a large bowl and cook on HIGH for 2 minutes, stirring occasionally. Add the vinegar and cook on HIGH for 3–5 minutes or until boiling.

2 Meanwhile, cut the cucumber and carrots into 0.5-cm ($\frac{1}{4}$-inch) slices, and break the cauliflower into tiny florets.

3 Add the vegetables to the boiling vinegar, cover and cook on HIGH for 2 minutes or until the liquid just returns to the boil. Once returned to the boil cook for a further 2 minutes.

4 Stir in the remaining ingredients and mix thoroughly together. Leave to cool, then pack into jars, cover and store in the refrigerator for up to 1 month, or pack into sterile jars and seal (see introduction).

HOT AND SPICY TOMATO CHUTNEY

This is a very quick chutney, not intended for storing, but to be made and eaten at once. Serve with nut or bean burgers. I like this combination of spices, but experiment with others such as cardamoms and caraway in place of the cumin and fenugreek.

► MAKES ABOUT 225 g ($\frac{1}{2}$ lb) ◄

45 ml (3 tbsp) vegetable oil
3 garlic cloves, skinned and crushed
2.5-cm (1-inch) piece root ginger, peeled and finely grated
5 ml (1 level tsp) ground turmeric
5 ml (1 level tsp) black mustard seeds
5 ml (1 level tsp) cumin seeds
5 ml (1 level tsp) coriander seeds
2.5 ml ($\frac{1}{2}$ level tsp) fenugreek seeds
1 red chilli, seeded and finely chopped
450 g (1 lb) ripe tomatoes, peeled and finely chopped
salt and pepper

1 Put the oil, garlic and ginger in a large bowl and cook on HIGH for 1–2 minutes, stirring once.

2 Meanwhile, grind the mustard seeds, cumin seeds, coriander seeds and fenugreek seeds in a pestle and mortar.

3 Stir all the spices into the oil and cook on HIGH for 1–2 minutes, or until the spices are sizzling, stirring once.

4 Add the chilli and the tomatoes and mix thoroughly together. Cook on HIGH for 10–12 minutes, or until most of the liquid has evaporated, stirring occasionally.

5 Season to taste with salt and pepper. Serve hot or cold. Store, covered, in the refrigerator for up to 2 weeks.

INDIAN SWEET CHUTNEY

Serve with very spicy Indian dishes or as a starter before a vegetable curry, Indian restaurant style; with poppadums, raita and a salad.

▶ MAKES ABOUT 450 g (1 lb) ◀

700 g (1½ lb) ripe tomatoes
30 ml (2 level tbsp) blanched almonds
100 g (4 oz) light muscovado sugar
4 garlic cloves, skinned and crushed
3 bay leaves
50 g (2 oz) sultanas
15 ml (1 level tbsp) nigella seeds
2.5 ml (½ level tsp) chilli powder
15 ml (3 fl oz) white wine vinegar
salt

1 Roughly chop the tomatoes and almonds and put into a large bowl. Add the remaining ingredients and cook on HIGH for 20 minutes or until slightly reduced and thickened.

2 Leave to cool then transfer to a clean jar or bowl, cover and store in the refrigerator for up to 2 weeks.

SWEETCORN RELISH

Use a large can of sweetcorn kernels, drained, in place of corn on the cob to make this a really quick relish.

▶ MAKES ABOUT 750 g (1½ lb) ◀

3 corn on the cob
2 medium onions, skinned and chopped
1 small green pepper, seeded and chopped
15 ml (1 tbsp) mild wholegrain mustard
5 ml (1 level tsp) ground turmeric
5 ml (1 level tsp) potato flour
100 g (4 oz) light muscovado sugar
300 ml (½ pint) white wine vinegar
salt

1 Remove the husk and the silk from the corn then wrap immediately in greaseproof paper. Cook on HIGH for 8–10 minutes or until tender, turning over half way through cooking. Strip the corn from the cob.

2 Put all the remaining ingredients into a large bowl and cook on HIGH for 5–7 minutes or until boiling, stirring once.

3 Add the corn to the rest of the ingredients and continue to cook on HIGH for 6–7 minutes until slightly reduced and thickened. Leave to cool, then transfer to a clean jar, cover and store in the refrigerator.

QUICK PICKLES, CHUTNEYS & RELISHES

PUDDINGS

The most successful microwave puddings range from one extreme to another, from old-fashioned, nursery-type puddings such as steamed or rice pudding to lightly cooked, fruit-based mousses or custards.

Fruits retain their colours and flavours, and like vegetables need only the minimum amount of water added to cook successfully. The rules for cooking vegetables apply when cooking fruits. Cut pieces into an even shape, stir during cooking and prick large whole fruits such as apples or pears. For a simple, healthy dessert, I'm very fond of baked apples. Remove the core and fill with dried fruit flavoured with a little ground cinnamon, nutmeg or coriander or fill with marzipan or nuts. Score the skin around the apple and place in a dish. Cook four apples on HIGH for about 5 minutes or until just soft to the touch. Poach four whole, peeled pears with a few tablespoons of orange juice on HIGH for about 5 minutes, or warm sliced bananas in orange juice, sweetened with a little honey or sugar on HIGH for 2–3 minutes for instant, fruity desserts.

Dried fruits cook well in the microwave and for extra flavour you can play around with the soaking liquid—try using tea or fruit juice and spices or wine or cider spiked with a dash of liqueur.

Steamed-type puddings are the other extreme. They rise before your eyes in only 5 minutes. If converting conventional suet puddings, use vegetarian suet.

KISSEL

Kissel was originally a Russian dessert. Consisting of red fruits in a liquid thickened with arrowroot, it is not quite a jelly, yet it has more body than fruit in syrup. For pure indulgence stir in a tablespoon of Cassis once the fruit has cooked.

▶ SERVES 4 ◀

30 ml (2 level tbsp) arrowroot
450 g (1 lb) mixed soft fruit, such as redcurrants, blackcurrants, raspberries, blackberries, bilberries, plums or cherries
15–30 ml (1–2 tbsp) runny honey

1 Put the arrowroot into a medium bowl and mix to a smooth paste with a little water. Gradually whisk in 150 ml ($\frac{1}{4}$ pint) of water.

2 Add all of the fruit except the raspberries, if using. Cover and cook on HIGH for 5 minutes or until the fruit has softened and the liquid has slightly thickened. Add the raspberries and cook on HIGH for 1 minute.

3 Spoon the Kissel into a serving dish, leave until cold, then chill for 2–3 hours before serving with Greek yogurt or smetana.

APPLE AND BLACKCURRANT CRUMBLE

This crumble has a rich, nutty texture and is far healthier than the conventional crumble as it contains little added sugar but gets most of its sweetness from coconut, nuts and sunflower seeds.

▶ SERVES 3–4 ◀

75 g (3 oz) butter or margarine
75 g (3 oz) plain wholemeal flour
25 g (1 oz) rolled oats
25 g (1 oz) sunflower seeds
15 g ($\frac{1}{2}$ oz) desiccated coconut
25 g (1 oz) chopped mixed nuts (optional)
25 g (1 oz) light muscovado sugar
5 ml (1 level tsp) ground cinnamon (optional)
2.5 ml ($\frac{1}{2}$ leve tsp) ground mixed spice (optional)
225 g (8 oz) eating apples, cored and sliced
225 g (8 oz) blackcurrants

1   Put the butter or margarine and flour into a bowl and rub together until the mixture resembles fine breadcrumbs. Stir in the dry ingredients and mix thoroughly together.

2   Put the apples and blackcurrants into a 1.1-litre (2-pint) deep dish. Spoon the crumble mixture evenly over the fruit and press down lightly. Cook, uncovered, on HIGH for 11–12 minutes or until the fruit is tender. Serve hot or cold with yogurt, cream or custard.

CHOCOLATE PECAN PIE

Not suitable for weight-watchers but most suitable for those who love sticky, rich chocolaty puddings with lots of calories! This is based on the traditional American pecan pie but instead of a pastry base it has a crunchy biscuit base. For real chocaholics try using plain chocolate digestives in place of the wholemeal digestive biscuits. If you cannot find pecan nuts, use walnut halves instead.

▶ MAKES 8 SLICES ◀

▶ *FOR THE BASE* ◀

100 g (4 oz) butter or margarine
225 g (8 oz) wholemeal digestive biscuits, finely crushed
75 g (3 oz) rolled oats

▶ *FOR THE FILLING* ◀

100 g (4 oz) chocolate, broken into small pieces
25 g (1 oz) butter or margarine
100 g (4 oz) dark muscovado sugar
60 ml (4 tbsp) golden syrup
175 g (6 oz) pecan nuts, roughly chopped
2 eggs

1 Grease a 20.5-cm (8-inch) fluted flan dish.

2 Put the butter or margarine in a medium bowl and cook on HIGH for 1–1½ minutes or until the butter has melted. Stir in the crushed biscuits and oats and mix together. Press evenly over the base of the flan dish.

3 To make the filling, put the chocolate, butter, sugar and golden syrup into a medium bowl and cook on HIGH for 1–2 minutes or until the chocolate has melted. Stir in the nuts and eggs and beat lightly together until well mixed.

4 Pour over the biscuit base. Stand on a roasting rack and cook on MEDIUM for 10–12 minutes or until the mixture is set. Serve cold, cut into wedges with thick yogurt or cream.

HOT FRUIT AND JASMINE SALAD

Dried fruit cooks quickly and successfully in the microwave oven, miraculously changing from dried, chewy lumps into plump, succulent fruits. Jasmine tea adds a delicious flavour and aroma, but experiment with other aromatic teas such as Earl Grey or fruit teas such as blackberry or passion fruit. Once cooked, the fruit in this salad is also delicious drained and topped with a crumble topping (see page 106). Stir a little of the jasmine-scented liquid into double cream or thick yogurt and serve as a sauce.

▶ SERVES 4–6 ◀

45 ml (3 tbsp) jasmine tea leaves
350 g (12 oz) mixed dried fruit, such as apricots, peaches, pears, apples and prunes
4 cloves
1 cinnamon stick
freshly grated nutmeg
½ a small lemon, thinly sliced

1 Make up the tea using 900 ml (1½ pints) of boiling water and leave to infuse for 5 minutes.

2 Put the fruit into a large bowl with the cloves, cinnamon stick, nutmeg and lemon slices.

3 Strain the tea over the fruit. Cover, and cook on HIGH for 15–20 minutes or until the fruit is tender. Serve hot or cold with thick natural yogurt.

FRANGIPAN TART

Frangipan was created in France during the reign of Louis XIII. It was originally a rich mixture of almonds or macaroons, eggs, sugar and flour used to fill cakes and pastries. My version contains macaroons and sugar, but the sauce is thickened with soya flour to add some protein. I have also included chopped candied peel or glacé fruit; try to use real candied peel bought from a good delicatessen rather than the unpleasant tasteless kind sold in pots in supermarkets.

▶ MAKES 8–12 SLICES ◀

▶ *FOR THE PASTRY CASE* ◀

75 g (6 oz) plain wholemeal flour
pinch of salt
75 g (3 oz) butter or margarine
30 ml (2 level tbsp) light muscovado sugar

▶ *FOR THE FILLING* ◀

50 g (2 oz) light muscovado sugar
50 g (2 oz) soya flour
450 ml ($\frac{3}{4}$ pint) milk
10 ml (2 level tsp) potato flour
100 g (4 oz) macaroons, finely crushed
a few drops of almond essence
100 g (4 oz) candied peel or glacé fruit, chopped
candied peel, glacé fruit, silver dragees, to decorate
icing sugar, to dredge

1 Grease a 20.5-cm (8-inch) fluted flan dish and line the base with greaseproof paper.

2 To make the pastry case, put the flour and salt in a bowl and rub in the butter or margarine until the mixture resembles fine breadcrumbs. Mix in the sugar. Add about 45 ml (3 tbsp) water to make a firm dough.

3 Turn on to a lightly-floured surface and knead for a few seconds until smooth. Roll out and use to line the base and sides of the prepared flan dish. Prick the base and sides with a fork.

4 Cover loosely with kitchen paper, stand on a roasting rack and cook on HIGH for 6–7 minutes or until the pastry is firm to the touch and just shrinking away from the sides of the dish.

5 Leave to stand for 2–3 minutes, then carefully remove the pastry case from the dish. Remove the greaseproof paper and place on a large flat plate.

6 To make the filling, put the sugar, soya flour and milk into a medium bowl and cook on HIGH for 5 minutes or until boiling, stirring once. Stir in the potato flour and cook on HIGH for 1–2 minutes until thickened, stirring occasionally. Add the macaroons, eggs and almond essence and mix thoroughly.

7   Arrange the candied peel or glacé fruit in the base of the pastry case and pour over the filling. Stand on a roasting rack and cook on MEDIUM for 10 minutes or until the mixture is set.

8   Leave to cool then decorate with glacé fruit and dredge lightly with icing sugar.

DATE AND WALNUT PUDDING WITH BRANDY SAUCE

An old-fashioned winter pudding, warming, nourishing and very filling! Sponge puddings of this type work very well in the microwave and never fail to amaze the uninitiated with the speed of cooking and the lightness of the result.

▶   SERVES 6–8   ◀

100 g (4 oz) softened butter or soft tub margarine
100 g (4 oz) light muscovado sugar
100 g (4 oz) self-raising wholemeal flour
5 ml (1 level tsp) ground mixed spice
2.5 ml ($\frac{1}{2}$ level tsp) ground cinnamon
2 eggs
60 ml (4 tbsp) milk
50 g (2 oz) walnut halves, finely chopped
50 g (2 oz) stoned dried dates, roughly chopped

▶   *FOR THE SAUCE*   ◀

20 g ($\frac{3}{4}$ oz) butter or margarine
20 g ($\frac{3}{4}$ oz) plain wholemeal flour
30 ml (2 level tbsp) light muscovado sugar
450 ml ($\frac{3}{4}$ pint) milk
45 ml (3 tbsp) brandy

1   Grease a 1.1-litre (2-pint) pudding basin and line the base with greaseproof paper.

2   Put the butter or margarine, sugar, flour, mixed spice, cinnamon, eggs and milk into a bowl and beat until smooth. Stir in the walnuts and dates.

3   Spoon the mixture into the prepared basin and level the surface. Cover loosely with kitchen paper then stand on a roasting rack and cook on HIGH for 5–6 minutes or well until risen and the sponge is shrinking away from the sides of the basin. Leave to stand for 5 minutes while making the brandy sauce.

4   To make the sauce, put all the ingredients in a medium bowl and blend well together. Cook on HIGH for 5–6 minutes or until boiling and thickened, stirring frequently. Stir in the brandy and cook on HIGH for a further 2 minutes.

5   Turn the pudding out on to a serving dish and serve immediately with the brandy sauce handed separately.

LAYERED FRUIT PUDDING

Suet puddings cook very successfully in the microwave because microwave cooking is similar to steaming. Vegetable suet is made from palm oil and can be substituted in any recipe calling for suet. The ideal covering for suet puddings in the microwave is clingfilm, but recently it has been suggested that clingfilm should be avoided in microwave cooking as the heat causes some of the chemicals in the clingfilm to migrate into the food. Non-PVC clingfilm is now available and claims to prevent this happening. I feel that as the case has not been proved one way or another, it is wise to cover with a plate.

▶ SERVES 6 ◀

▶ *FOR THE PASTRY* ◀

100 g (4 oz) self-raising flour
100 g (4 oz) self-raising wholemeal flour
15 ml (1 level tbsp) light muscovado sugar
100 g (4 oz) vegetable suet
finely grated rind and juice of half a lemon

▶ *FOR THE FILLING* ◀

finely grated rind and juice of 1 lemon
225 g (8 oz) eating apples
225 g (8 oz) ripe plums
30–60 ml (2–4 level tbsp) light muscovado sugar
225 g (8 oz) raspberries or blackberries

1   Grease a 1.4-litre (2½-pint) pudding basin or bowl and line the base with a circle of greaseproof paper.

2   To make the pastry, put the flours, sugar, suet and lemon rind in a bowl, then mix with the lemon juice and about 70 ml (6 tbsp) water to make a soft, but not sticky, dough.

3   Turn the dough out on to a lightly floured surface and shape into a cylinder, wider at one end than the other. Cut into 4 pieces.

4   Shape the smallest piece of pastry into a round, large enough to fit the bottom of the pudding basin. Press into the bottom of the basin.

5   Peel the apples, if liked, and remove the core. Cut into thin slices then put in the bowl on top of the pastry. Sprinkle with the lemon rind and juice.

6   Shape the next smallest piece of pastry into a round and place on top of the apples. Halve the plums and remove the stones and place on top of the pastry. Sprinkle with sugar to taste.

7   Shape a third piece of pastry into a round and place on top of the plums. Spoon the raspberries or blackberries on top. Shape the remaining pastry into a round large enough to cover the raspberries and place on top making sure that the pastry fits right to the edges of the bowl.

8   Push the pastry down with your hand to compress the layers slightly and allow space for the pudding to rise during cooking.

9   Cover and cook on HIGH for 14–15 minutes or until the top layer of pastry feels firm to the touch. Leave to stand, covered, for 5 minutes, then turn out and serve immediately with yogurt, cream or custard.

FRUIT AND POLENTA PUDDING

Polenta is usually a savoury dish, flavoured with cheese, rather like Gnocchi (see page 64). But here it is combined successfully with lemon, raisins and honey to make an unusual and nutritious dessert, rather similar to a chilled cheesecake. See the photograph facing page 97.

▶   SERVES 6   ◀

600 ml (1 pint) milk
100 g (4 oz) cornmeal
100 g (4 oz) raisins
25 g (1 oz) butter or margarine
30 ml (2 tbsp) runny honey
a few drops of vanilla essence
finely grated rind and juice of 1 lemon
fresh fruit, such as star fruit, strawberries, kiwi fruit, raspberries, apricots, mangoes, prepared and sliced

▶   *FOR THE GLAZE*   ◀

30 ml (2 tbsp) apricot jam
lemon juice

1   Grease a 23-cm (9-inch) square dish and line the base with greaseproof paper.

2   Put the milk into a large bowl and cook on HIGH for 4–5 minutes or until hot but not boiling. Gradually stir in the cornmeal and mix thoroughly together. Cook on HIGH for 5–6 minutes or until very thick, stirring frequently.

3   Stir in the raisins, butter, honey, vanilla essence, lemon rind and juice and mix well together. Pour into the prepared dish and level the surface. Leave for 2–3 hours or until set.

4   Turn the polenta out on to a flat surface and cut into six pieces. Arrange the fruit attractively on top.

5   To make the glaze, put the jam and a squeeze of lemon juice in a small bowl and cook on HIGH for 20–30 seconds or until the jam has melted. Brush over the fruit to glaze.

FRESH FRUIT TRIFLE

I often feel like making (and eating!) a rich trifle with a gooey sponge base soaked in alcohol, topped with fruit and cream, but, alas, never have a spare sponge to turn into such a creation. However, with the aid of a microwave you can cook a sponge in just 5–6 minutes, then instantly (generously!) transform it into a trifle! I prefer to omit the traditional custard topping and instead mix tofu with cream to make a thick, rich layer. If you prefer omit the tofu and double the quantity of cream.

▶ SERVES 6 ◀

▶ *FOR THE SPONGE* ◀

100 g (4 oz) softened butter or soft tub margarine

100 g (4 oz) light muscovado sugar

50 g (2 oz) self-raising wholemeal flour

50 g (2 oz) self-raising flour

2 eggs

30 ml (2 tbsp) milk

▶ *FOR THE FILLING* ◀

90 ml (6 tbsp) pear and apple spread or raspberry or apricot jam

150 ml ($\frac{1}{4}$ pint) sherry, Madeira or Marsala

100 ml (4 fl oz) unsweetened apple juice

225 g (8 oz) raspberries

225 g (8 oz) grapes, halved and deseeded

1 kiwi fruit, peeled and chopped

▶ *FOR THE TOPPING* ◀

100 g (4 oz) silken tofu

300 ml ($\frac{1}{2}$ pint) double cream

60 ml (4 tbsp) ground almonds

30 ml (2 tbsp) almonds, toasted (see page 31)

1 Grease a 20.5-cm (8-inch) round dish and line the base with greaseproof paper.

2 To make the sponge, put the butter or margarine, sugar, flour, eggs and milk in a bowl and beat until smooth.

3 Spoon into the prepared dish and level the surface. Cover, stand on a roasting rack and cook on HIGH for 5–6 minutes or until risen and slightly shrunk away from the sides of the dish.

4 Uncover and leave to stand for 5 minutes, then turn out and leave to cool on a wire rack. When completely cold, cut in half horizontally, then sandwich together with the pear and apple spread.

5 Cut into 5-cm (2-inch) pieces and arrange in the bottom of a large glass serving dish.

6 Mix the sherry and apple juice together and pour over the sponge. Arrange the fruit evenly on top.

Fig and Honey Ramekins, page 115

7   To make the topping put the tofu and double cream in a food processor or blender and process until smooth. Stir in the ground almonds. Spoon evenly over the fruit and level the surface. Sprinkle with the toasted almonds. Chill for 2–3 hours before serving.

STRAWBERRY AND MANGO RING

Choosing a good, ripe mango is not easy since there are many varieties that vary in colour—so do not choose by colour. Instead, pick up the fruit and squeeze it gently, if it gives then it is ripe. You can also go by the smell; when ripe they have a delicious fruity aroma. Preparing mangoes is also a bit tricky unless you understand the anatomy of the fruit. Inside it contains a large flat oval-shaped stone. The easiest way to deal with this is to cut either side of the stone and then scrape the remaining flesh away from the stone.

▸   SERVES 6   ◂

2 ripe mangoes
60 ml (4 level tbsp) agar-agar flakes
450 ml (¾ pint) Greek yogurt
finely grated rind and juice of 1 lime
45 ml (3 tbsp) runny honey
2 egg whites
225 g (8 oz) strawberries

1   Using a sharp knife slice either side of the central stone. Roughly chop the flesh, discarding the skin. Scrape the mango flesh from the central stone. Put half of the chopped mango in a food processor or blender with the yogurt, half of the lime rind and juice and honey and purée until smooth. Turn into a bowl.

2   Put the agar-agar flakes in a small bowl with 300 ml (½ pint) water and leave to soak for 15 minutes. Cook on HIGH for 3 minutes or until boiling then continue to cook on HIGH for 2 minutes or until the agar-agar has dissolved, stirring occasionally.

3   Stir into the mango and yogurt mixture with the remaining chopped mango. Whisk the egg whites until stiff and fold into the mixture.

4   Wet a 1.1-litre (2-pint) ring mould and spoon in the mango and yogurt mousse. Level the surface, then chill for about 3–4 hours or until set.

5   To serve, turn the mousse out on to a serving plate. Mix the remaining lime rind and juice with the strawberries and pile into the centre of the ring.

PUDDINGS

Herb, Cheese and Olive Bread, page 117; Mushroom, Courgette and Bean Stew, page 88

ORANGE SABAYON

This is a delicious creamy mixture, something of a cross between a mousse and a frothy sauce, but it is served warm. It is easier to achieve the desired, light fluffy consistency if you use an electric whisk. However, if you do not own one, a balloon whisk and a lot of elbow power will do! Make sure that you grate the orange rind very finely or the flavour will be spoilt by large bitter pieces of rind.

► SERVES 2 ◄

2 egg yolks
50 g (2 oz) light muscovado sugar
finely grated rind and juice of 1 orange
30 ml (2 tbsp) orange liqueur
crisp biscuits, such as tuiles or langues de chat, to serve

1 Put the eggs and sugar in a bowl and whisk with an electric whisk until thick and pale.

2 Gradually whisk in the orange rind and juice and the liqueur. Cook on HIGH for 1 minute then whisk again.

3 Cook on HIGH for 45 seconds–1 minute or until the mixture sets very slightly around the edge of the bowl. (Do not overcook or the egg will scramble.)

4 Whisk again. The mixture should just leave a trail when the whisk is lifted. Pour into two tall glasses or dishes and serve immediately with biscuits. The self-indulgent might like to top the warm sabayon with a spoonful of thick double cream and a few toasted nuts, delicious!

CHOCOLATE AND PEAR CUSTARDS

Use a firm ripe pear such as Conference to make these, other varieties such as Williams or Packham are so soft and juicy when ripe that they disintegrate during cooking and spoil the texture of the custard. Leave them in the ramekin dishes to serve, or turn out so that the square of dark, rich chocolate is revealed.

► SERVES 6 ◄

2 medium ripe pears
100 g (4 oz) dark chocolate or plain carob bar
5 ml (1 level tsp) cocoa or carob powder
15 ml (1 level tbsp) dark muscovado sugar
300 ml ($\frac{1}{2}$ pint) milk or a mixture of milk and single cream
1 egg
1 egg yolk

► *TO SERVE* ◄

2 medium ripe pears
5 ml (1 level tsp) icing sugar
5 ml (1 level tsp) cocoa or carob powder

PUDDINGS

1   Peel and core the pear, chop roughly and divide between 4 ramekin dishes. Break the chocolate or carob into squares and put 1 square into each dish on top of the pear.

2   Put the remaining chocolate or carob, cocoa or carob powder, sugar and the milk in a jug or small bowl and cook on HIGH for 2–3 minutes or until the chocolate or carob has melted, stirring occasionally. Stir in the egg, and egg yolk and beat thoroughly together. Carefully pour the mixture on top of the pear. Arrange the ramekins in a circle in the oven and cook on LOW for just 15 minutes or until the custards are just set. Cool, then chill for at least 2 hours before serving.

3   To serve, peel the remaining pear if liked and cut into neat slices. Arrange the custards on individual plates with the sliced pears. Dust the top of each custard with the icing sugar and the pears with cocoa or carob powder. Serve immediately. These are best eaten on the day of making.

FIG AND HONEY RAMEKINS

Use the large dried figs that are sold loose rather than the type compressed into a large block to make these, as they have a much better shape and texture.
See the photograph facing page 112.

▶   SERVES 4   ◀

about 20 dried figs

▶   FOR THE FILLING   ◀
175 g (6 oz) curd cheese
50 g (2 oz) shelled pistachio nuts, finely chopped
50 g (2 oz) no-soak apricots, finely chopped
15 ml (1 tbsp) runny honey
15 ml (1 tbsp) brandy

▶   FOR THE SAUCE   ◀
60 ml (4 tbsp) runny honey
15 ml (1 tbsp) brandy
chopped shelled pistachio nuts, to decorate

1   Put the figs into a large bowl and pour over enough boiling water to cover. Cover and cook on HIGH for 5–7 minutes or until softened.

2   To make the filling, put the cheese, nuts, apricots, honey and brandy into a bowl and beat together.

3   Grease four ramekin dishes. Split the figs down one side if necessary, to open them out flat. Use 5 figs to line the base and sides of each ramekin, arranging them skin side outwards. Fill each dish with the cheese mixture. Level the surface, cover and chill for at least 4 hours.

4   When ready to serve, make the sauce. Put the honey and brandy in a small bowl and cook on HIGH for $1-1\frac{1}{2}$ minutes or until just hot. To serve, turn out on to 4 plates and sprinkle with chopped pistachio nuts. Serve with the hot brandy sauce.

QUICK BREADS & BAKING

Cakes and breads cooked in the microwave will not brown and crisp as when conventionally baked, but including ingredients like wholemeal flour adds colour and means that the result is healthier too.

Because breads cook so quickly, it seems pointless to use yeast as the raising agent. The breads included here are quick breads using quick-acting self-raising flour, baking powder or bicarbonate of soda as raising agents. All baked goods benefit from being cooked on a microwave roasting rack, so that the microwaves can penetrate the food from the underneath too. If you do not own a roasting rack, use an upturned bowl instead. Although this is not as effective it provides a better result than when the cake, bread or teabread is cooked standing in contact with the base of the oven.

Microwave-baked goods have a reputation for being dry. If you include ingredients such as cheese, buttermilk or apple, or more unusual ingredients such as beetroot or courgettes, they help keep cakes or teabreads moist and have the added benefit of adding colour, flavour, texture and nutrients.

These breads are so quick to make that it is easy to cook them just before serving so you can enjoy eating them while they are still warm. They do keep well for 1–2 days if you wrap them in greaseproof paper and foil if you want to eat them fresh, or for up to 4 days to eat toasted.

Cakes will keep for 2–3 days if stored in an airtight container.

IRISH SODA BREAD

Soda bread is quick to cook conventionally, but this microwaved version is so good that you could convince your friends that it was baked in a conventional oven. Serve warm in chunks with homemade soup or slice and serve with salads or stews.

► MAKES 1 LARGE LOAF (18 SLICES) ◄

450 g (1 lb) self-raising wholemeal flour plus extra for sprinkling
225 g (8 oz) plain flour
salt
2.5 ml ($\frac{1}{2}$ level tsp) bicarbonate of soda
600 ml (1 pint) buttermilk

1   Put the flours, salt to taste and bicarbonate of soda in a large bowl and mix together.

2   Pour in the buttermilk and mix quickly to form a soft dough. Knead lightly on a floured surface and shape into a 25-cm (10-inch) round cob loaf. Cut a large cross in the top, and dust lightly with a little wholemeal flour.

3   Place the loaf on a microwave baking tray and stand on a roasting rack. Cook on HIGH for 15 minutes or until risen and firm to the touch. Serve warm, or cool on a wire rack and eat within 2 days.

HERB, CHEESE AND OLIVE BREAD

This makes a moist, quick bread, delicious served warm or cold with soups or salads. Use a strong Cheddar cheese and juicy black olives packed in olive oil for the best flavour. Fresh herbs such as oregano, marjoram or rosemary complement the flavour of cheese and olives. See the photograph facing page 113.

► MAKES 1 LOAF (16 SLICES) ◄

225 g (8 oz) self-raising wholemeal flour
5 ml (1 level tsp) baking powder
salt and pepper
100 g (4 oz) mature Cheddar cheese, grated
45 ml (3 tbsp) roughly chopped fresh mixed herbs
75 g (3 oz) black olives, quartered
1 egg
30 ml (2 tbsp) olive oil
225 ml (8 fl oz) milk

► FOR THE TOPPING ◄
25 g (1 oz) mature Cheddar cheese, grated
15 ml (1 tbsp) roughly chopped fresh mixed herbs
25 g (1 oz) black olives, roughly chopped

1   Grease a 1.7-litre (3-pint) loaf dish and line the base with greaseproof paper.

2   Put the flour, baking powder, salt and pepper, cheese, herbs, black olives, egg, olive oil and milk in a large bowl and beat thoroughly until well mixed.

3   Spoon the mixture into the prepared dish and level the surface. Sprinkle on the topping. Stand the container on a roasting rack and cook on HIGH for 3 minutes then continue to cook on MEDIUM for 14 minutes or until firm to the touch and well risen.

4   Leave to cool in the dish. When cold turn out and serve sliced, spread with a little butter or margarine.

CHILLI CORN BREAD

Cornmeal, which is as the name suggests, ground corn, gives this bread a bright yellow colour and a distinctive flavour and texture. Don't be surprised by the addition of sugar, it helps to bring out the flavour but still produces a savoury bread. Omit the chillies if you prefer but they do give a certain punch and add attractive flecks of green to the bread (see the photograph facing page 96).

► MAKES 8 PIECES ◄

75 g (3 oz) butter or margarine
100 g (4 oz) plain flour
100 g (4 oz) cornmeal
15 ml (1 level tbsp) baking powder
45 ml (3 level tbsp) light muscovado sugar
1–2 green chillies, seeded and chopped
salt
1 egg, beaten
150 ml ($\frac{1}{4}$ pint) milk

1 Grease a 23 × 12.5-cm (9 × 5-inch) dish and line the base with greaseproof paper.

2 Put the butter or margarine in a large bowl and cook on HIGH for 1–1$\frac{1}{2}$ minutes until melted.

3 Add the remaining ingredients and beat thoroughly until well mixed.

4 Spoon the mixture into the prepared dish and level the surface. Cover with kitchen paper, stand on a roasting rack and cook on HIGH for 5 minutes until well risen, firm to the touch but still moist in the middle.

5 Leave to cool in the dish. When cold, turn out and cut into 8 pieces. Serve with soup or Mexican Chilli Beans (see page 86).

ZAHTER BREAD

Zahter is a mixture of sesame seeds, marjoram, thyme and lemon rind, used in Middle Eastern cooking to flavour salads, breads and stews. It can be made in a greater quantity than here and stored in a screw-top jar until needed. Here it is mixed with butter and used to flavour a bought loaf. Serve instead of garlic bread for a pleasant change.

► SERVES 4–6 ◄

100 g (4 oz) butter or margarine
5 ml (1 tsp) sesame seeds
5 ml (1 level tsp) ground dried marjoram
5 ml (1 level tsp) ground dried thyme
5 ml (1 tsp) grated lemon rind
salt
1 large granary round

1   Put the butter or margarine in a medium bowl and cook on HIGH for 30–60 seconds or until just soft enough to beat.

2   Add the sesame seeds, marjoram, thyme, lemon rind and salt to taste and beat together until well mixed.

3   Cut the bread into 2.5-cm (1-inch) slices, cutting almost through to the base. Repeat the 2.5-cm (1-inch) slices at right angles to the first slices to make small square columns of bread still attached to the base.

4   Spread all the cut sides of the squares of bread with the Zahter butter. Wrap the granary round in greaseproof paper and cook on HIGH for 2–3 minutes or until just warm. Serve immediately.

COURGETTE TEABREAD

Grated courgettes give this teabread an interesting speckled green appearance and keep it moist. Serve sliced and buttered as a savoury bread with soups or salads, or increase the honey to 15 ml (3 tbsp) and sprinkle the top lightly with a little icing sugar and mixed spice and serve as an alternative sweet teabread.

▶   MAKES 12 SLICES   ◀

225 g (8 oz) plain wholemeal flour
75 g (3 oz) plain flour
5 ml (1 level tsp) baking powder
1.25 ml ($\frac{1}{4}$ level tsp) ground mace
1.25 ml ($\frac{1}{4}$ level tsp) ground mixed spice
finely grated rind of $\frac{1}{2}$ an orange
salt
150 ml ($\frac{1}{4}$ pint) natural yogurt
15 ml (1 tbsp) runny honey
60 ml (4 tbsp) milk
2 eggs
225 g (8 oz) courgettes, grated
75 g (3 oz) cashew nuts, chopped

1   Grease a 1.7-litre (3-pint) loaf dish and line the base with greaseproof paper.

2   Put the flours, baking powder, mace, mixed spice and orange rind in a large bowl, mix well together and add salt to taste.

3   Beat in the yogurt, honey, milk and the eggs. Reserve a handful of the courgettes and a few nuts for decoration and add the remainder. Beat together thoroughly. Spoon the mixture into the loaf dish and level the surface. Sprinkle the reserved nuts and courgettes on top.

4   Stand on a roasting rack and cook on HIGH for 3 minutes, then on MEDIUM for 18 minutes or until well risen and firm to the touch.

5   Serve warm or turn out on to a cooling rack and leave to cool. Courgette teabread will keep wrapped in foil for 1–2 days.

NUTTY VEGAN BARS

These fibre-packed bars contain no animal products and no added sugar. They keep well, wrapped in foil, for up to one week.

▶ MAKES 12 BARS ◀

450 g (1 lb) eating apples, peeled, cored and finely chopped
75 ml (5 tbsp) unsweetened apple, orange or pineapple juice
225 g (8 oz) mixed dried fruit such as ready-to-eat apricots, dates, sultanas
100 g (4 oz) chopped mixed nuts
75 g (3 oz) rolled oats
75 g (3 oz) self-raising wholemeal flour
25 g (1 oz) desiccated coconut
50 g (2 oz) pumpkin seeds
30 ml (2 tbsp) vegetable oil
30 ml (2 tbsp) pear and apple spread

1   Put the apples and the fruit juice in a large bowl, cover and cook on HIGH for 5–6 minutes or until the apple is very soft, stirring occasionally. Beat thoroughly to make a smooth purée.

2   Chop the dried fruit if large then add to the purée with the remaining ingredients and beat well together. Spoon into a 20.5 × 20.5-cm (8 × 8-inch) dish and level the surface. Stand on a roasting rack and cook on MEDIUM for 10–12 minutes or until firm to the touch.

3   Put the pear and apple spread into a small bowl and cook on HIGH for 20–30 seconds until just warm. Brush evenly over the mixture.

4   Mark into 12 bars while still warm, then leave to cool in the dish. When cold turn out and cut into bars.

SPICY APPLE CAKE

This very moist cake is equally good served warm as a dessert with custard, cream or yogurt. I have included mixed spice and ground cinnamon to make a spicy cake, but if you prefer you can omit them and add a little finely grated lemon rind instead.

▶ MAKES 16 SLICES ◀

450 g (1 lb) cooking apples, peeled, cored and roughly chopped
225 g (8 oz) plain wholemeal flour
10 ml (2 level tsp) baking powder
5 ml (1 level tsp) ground mixed spice
2.5 ml ($\frac{1}{2}$ level tsp) ground cinnamon
100 g (4 oz) softened butter or soft tub margarine
175 g (6 oz) light muscovado sugar
2 eggs
75 ml (5 tbsp) milk
icing sugar, to dredge

1   Grease a 1.6-litre (2¾-pint) ring mould and scatter a third of the apple in the base.

2   Put the flour, baking powder, spices, butter or margarine, sugar and milk in a bowl and beat until smooth.

3   Fold in the remaining apple then spoon the cake mixture into the ring mould and level the surface.

4   Cook on HIGH for 8–9 minutes or until the cake is well risen, firm to the touch and no longer looks wet around the centre edge. Leave to cool in the dish then turn out and dredge with icing sugar. Spicy Apple Cake will keep for 1–2 days in an airtight container.

WALNUT, BANANA AND ORANGE TEABREAD

Bananas keep this teabread moist and add a delicious flavour; make sure that you mash them well before mixing with the other ingredients. As I am a great chocolate fan, I like to use it wherever possible, so I sometimes add 30 ml (2 tbsp) cocoa powder and a little milk to make a chocolate banana loaf.

▶   MAKES 16 SLICES   ◀

225 g (8 oz) self-raising wholemeal flour
100 g (4 oz) light muscovado sugar
100 g (4 oz) butter or margarine
100 g (4 oz) walnut halves, roughly chopped
3 ripe bananas, mashed
1 egg
finely grated rind and juice of 1 large orange
2.5 ml (½ level tsp) ground mixed spice

▶   *FOR THE TOPPING*   ◀

25 g (1 oz) walnut halves
25 g (1 oz) dried banana chips
15 ml (1 tbsp) runny honey

1   Grease a 1.7-litre (3-pint) loaf dish and line with greaseproof paper.

2   Put the flour, sugar, butter, walnuts, bananas, egg, orange rind and juice and mixed spice in a large bowl and beat thoroughly until well mixed.

3   Spoon the mixture into the prepared dish and level the surface. Sprinkle with the walnuts and banana chips. Stand on a roasting rack and cook on MEDIUM for 14 minutes or until well risen and firm to the touch.

4   Leave to cool in the dish. When cold turn out and brush with the honey to glaze. Serve sliced, plain or spread with a little butter or margarine. Walnut, Banana and Orange Teabread will keep wrapped in foil for 1–2 days.

BEETROOT CAKE

Beetroot not only gives this cake a wonderful colour, but sweetens it, allowing the sugar to be greatly reduced, and helps to keep it moist. If buying beetroot already cooked, make sure that it has not been steeped in vinegar or brine, or the cake will have an unintentional added flavour!

To cook beetroot in the microwave, prick the skin all over with a fork and then put in a medium bowl with 30 ml (2 tbsp) water. Cover and cook on HIGH for 10–12 minutes or until tender and the skins rub off easily.

▶ MAKES 12 SLICES ◀

225 g (8 oz) cooked, peeled, beetroot
50 g (2 oz) light muscovado sugar
finely grated rind of 1 lemon
2.5 ml ($\frac{1}{2}$ level tsp) ground cinnamon
225 g (8 oz) self-raising wholemeal flour
5 ml (1 level tsp) baking powder
100 g (4 oz) butter or margarine
2 eggs

▶ *FOR THE ICING* ◀

100 g (4 oz) cream cheese
25–50 g (1–2 oz) icing sugar
juice of half a lemon
15 g ($\frac{1}{2}$ oz) flaked almonds

1   Grease a deep 20.5-cm (8-inch) round cake dish and line the base with greaseproof paper.

2   Put the beetroot, sugar, lemon rind, cinnamon and 15 ml (1 tbsp) water in a blender or food processor and purée until smooth.

3   Add the flour, baking powder and butter or margarine and process until well mixed. Turn the mixture into the prepared dish and level the surface.

4   Stand on a roasting rack, cover and cook on HIGH for 5 minutes, then on MEDIUM for 4–5 minutes, or until well risen but still slightly moist on the surface. Leave to cool in the dish.

5   To make the icing, beat the cheese, icing sugar and lemon juice together until smooth and creamy.

6   Turn the cake out on to a serving plate. Using a palette knife, spread the icing over the top of the cake.

7   Spread the almonds out on a baking sheet or large flat plate and cook on HIGH for 4–6 minutes or until lightly browned. Sprinkle on top of the cake.

LEMONY COCONUT CAKE

This is the basic recipe and method for cooking a sponge in the microwave. If you intend to cook lots of cakes it is worth buying a plastic roasting rack to stand the cake on during cooking, as it allows the microwaves to cook deep cakes from underneath as well as from the sides, so that the cooking time is reduced and the cake remains moist.

▶ MAKES 8 SLICES ◀

175 g (6 oz) softened butter or soft tub margarine
175 g (6 oz) light muscovado sugar
75 g (3 oz) self-raising flour
75 g (3 oz) self-raising wholemeal flour
3 eggs
finely grated rind and juice of 3 lemons
45 ml (3 tbsp) lemon curd

▶ *FOR THE TOPPING* ◀

2 eggs, separated
100 g (4 oz) desiccated coconut
30 ml (2 tbsp) runny honey
30 ml (2 tbsp) shredded coconut

1   Grease a deep 20.5-cm (8-inch) round dish and line the base with greaseproof paper.

2   Put the butter or margarine, sugar, flours, eggs, lemon rind and all but 15 ml (1 tbsp) of the juice into a bowl. Beat until smooth.

3   Spoon the mixture into the prepared dish and level the surface. Cover, stand on a roasting rack and cook on HIGH for 6–7 minutes or until it has risen and slightly shrunk away from the sides of the dish.

4   Uncover and leave to stand for 5 minutes, then turn out and leave to cool on a wire rack.

5   When completely cold, spread the lemon curd over the top of the cake.

6   To make the topping, put the egg yolks, desiccated coconut, honey and reserved lemon juice into a bowl and mix well together. Whisk the egg whites until stiff and fold into the coconut mixture. Spoon evenly over the lemon curd and sprinkle with the shredded coconut.

7   Brown the top evenly under a preheated grill then leave to cool. Best eaten within two days.

CHOCOLATE AND ALMOND CAKE

This rich, moist chocolate cake resembles the famous Austrian Sachertorte in its beginning, but instead of a chocolate covering, it is topped with a nutritious marzipan paste made from soya flour and ground almonds. The almonds can be omitted altogether and replaced by soya flour if you wish to reduce the cost. Melted chocolate and flaked almonds complete the cake, which is delicious and presentable enough to be served for a special occasion.

▶ MAKES 12 SLICES ◀

100 g (4 oz) plain chocolate, or plain carob bar, broken into small pieces
100 g (4 oz) softened butter or soft tub margarine
100 g (4 oz) dark muscovado sugar
100 g (4 oz) ground almonds
4 eggs, separated
50 g (2 oz) fresh brown breadcrumbs
30 ml (2 tbsp) apricot jam
15 ml (1 tbsp) Amaretto di Saronno (optional)

▶ FOR THE MARZIPAN ◀

75 g (3 oz) ground almonds
75 g (3 oz) soya flour
30 ml (2 tbsp) runny honey
1 egg white
lemon juice
almond essence

▶ FOR THE DECORATION ◀

175 g (6 oz) plain chocolate or carob bar
50 g (2 oz) toasted flaked almonds (see page 31)

1 Grease a 25.5-cm (10-inch) round dish that is about 2.5 cm (1 inch) deep and line the base with greaseproof paper.

2 Put the chocolate in a small bowl and cook on LOW for 4–5 minutes. Stir until melted.

3 Cream the butter or margarine and sugar together until soft and fluffy. Stir in the almonds, egg yolks, breadcrumbs and melted chocolate and beat until well mixed.

4 Whisk the egg whites until stiff then pour in the chocolate mixture and carefully fold together. Pour into the prepared dish and level the surface.

5 Cook on MEDIUM for 10–11 minutes until just shrinking away from the edges and almost firm in the centre.

6 Meanwhile, make the marzipan. Put the almonds and soya flour in a bowl and mix together. Make a well in the centre then add the honey, egg white and lemon juice and almond essence to taste. Mix together, using your fingers, to make a stiff dough. Knead lightly, then form into a ball and cover until required.

7   Leave the cake to cool in the dish, then turn out on to a wire rack and leave to cool. When cool, mix the apricot jam with the Amaretto if using, and brush over the top and sides of the cake.

8   Roll out the marzipan on a surface dusted with a little soya flour to a circle large enough to cover the top of the cake. Place on top of the cake and press down lightly so that it sticks.

9   Put the chocolate for the decoration in a medium bowl and cook on LOW for 6–8 minutes. Stir until melted. Spread some of the chocolate around the side of the cake to coat completely. Spoon the remainder into a small piping bag fitted with a plain nozzle and pipe on top of the cake in a squiggle pattern.

10   Press the almonds round the sides of the cake and sprinkle a few on top. Leave to cool then transfer to a large flat serving plate. Chocolate and Almond Cake will keep for 2–3 days in an airtight container or wrapped in foil.

BRAN AND RAISIN MUFFINS

Muffins have recently become very popular in this country. They are quick to make and rise like magic in just 5 minutes when cooked in the microwave. Serve them for tea or for breakfast, mixing the dry ingredients together the night before, and then adding the egg, milk and honey in the morning just before cooking. You can experiment at your leisure by adding other ingredients such as chocolate or dried fruits. Try chopped fresh fruit or whole, soft fruits such as raspberries, blackcurrants or bilberries, or chopped nuts. Or omit the honey and add a few chopped fresh mixed herbs, tiny cubes of Cheddar or hard cheese and a tablespoonful of vegetable oil.

► MAKES 8 MUFFINS ◄

50 g (2 oz) bran
75 g (3 oz) self-raising wholemeal flour
5 ml (1 level tsp) baking powder
1 egg
300 ml ($\frac{1}{2}$ pint) milk
30 ml (2 tbsp) runny honey
50 g (2 oz) raisins

1   Put all the ingredients in a large bowl and beat thoroughly together.

2   Divide the mixture into 8 rounds and place in an 8-hole muffin tray and cook on HIGH for 5–6 minutes or until firm to the touch.

3   Leave to stand for 5 minutes then turn out and serve warm, either plain or split and buttered.

INDEX